# Year-Round Schools

*The Abt Associates Series in Social Policy Analysis*

# Year-Round Schools

**Morris A. Shepard**
Abt Associates, Inc.

**Keith Baker**
Department of Health, Education,
and Welfare

**Lexington Books**
D.C. Heath and Company
Lexington, Massachusetts
Toronto

**Library of Congress Cataloging in Publication Data**

Shepard, Morris A.
   Year-round schools.

   Bibliography: p.
   1. School year. I. Baker, Keith, joint author. II. Title.
LB3034.S53        371.2'36      76-50491
ISBN 0-669-01285-8

International Standard Book Number: 76-50491

Library of Congress Catalog Card Number: 0-669-01285-8

Abt Associates Inc., with headquarters in Cambridge, Massachusetts, is the largest social science research firm in the United States. Its staff of 700 includes social scientists from various disciplines: anthropology, economics, psychology, sociology, statistics. Their expertise is combined in interdisciplinary applied social research projects, primarily under contract to federal governmental agencies.

# Contents

# List of Figures

# List of Tables

# Preface

Our purpose is to provide the best available information about year-round schools (YRS) to those thinking about YRS as an educational option for their community. Parents, teachers, students, and administrators will find the experiences of other communities helpful, even though some of the information is speculative and the conclusions tentative. Better decisions can be reached when decision makers are aware of the experiences of others.

The information we offer includes a concise history of YRS in America and a wide range of case studies of real communities that have ventured to change their school calendar. We discuss some of the many issues that can be involved in such a change, and we express views about the involvement of the federal government in YRS.

While we are enthusiastic about the experiences and information that we have analyzed and that we report here, we do not wish to be viewed as YRS advocates. YRS is not an educational panacea. Rather, like hybrid corn, YRS grows and flourishes in some settings and not in others. Advocating its widespread adoption would be premature; too many YRS issues remain unstudied. Systematically derived answers are especially needed for the pressing questions of academic effectiveness and costs.

A number of people helped in collecting and analyzing the information, and in some instances drafted chapters of an earlier related work: they are Pat Griffin, Gerald Goldman, Julia Shepard, Mary Reed, and Gerald Vigneron. Paul Rice, David Parks, Johannes Olsen, and Donald Parks shared with us their ideas for classifying and graphically representing the different YRS calendars outlined in Chapter 1. Peter Desmond judiciously edited and Gale Halpern skillfully typed the manuscript. While this work is based on two studies carried out for the Department of Health, Education, and Welfare by Abt Associates, Inc. (HEW-100-75-0013) and the National Council of Year-Round Education (HEW-4997-75), it does not necessarily reflect the policy or opinion of DHEW. The responsibility for conclusions and opinions offered here is solely ours.

Morris A. Shepard
Winchester, Massachusetts, 1976

Keith Baker
Washington, D.C., 1976

# Year-Round Schools

# 1

# Year-Round Schools from the 1800s to the Present

Almost one million American students in more than one hundred school districts are going to schools that operate "year round." Another one hundred school districts are considering year-round schools (YRS)—thus another million children could soon be affected. Are these children then going to school for twelve months out of the year? Not at all; unless they choose otherwise, they probably attend classes no more than 180 days a year, like their peers at schools that employ the traditional school calendar. However, they attend school at different times of year. Summer vacation, with its vacant school buildings and teachers on unemployment or moonlighting at menial jobs, is not part of YRS. Instead, YRS teachers hold regular classes over the summer in buildings that are used to full capacity.

Going to school year round means different things in different communities. Generally speaking, some portion of the students are attending year-round schools throughout the year. But different communities have divided their YRS program into three, four, five, or six equal parts, and students are required to attend two, three, or four of the school calendar parts in order to meet the 180-day attendance requirement.

Tinkering with the traditional school calendar of September to June may seem like a new and unnecessary idea, but it is neither. Americans have been adjusting the school calendar for more than a century, and it looks as though the end of innovation is not in sight. These YRS variations are being developed by people trying to economize scarce tax dollars and make the educational system more flexible.

The brief history of year-round schools that follows outlines the evolution and variation of YRS programs in the United States. First, however, we define three major types of extended calendars.

Since the 180-day "traditional" school year was developed, three major exceptions to this school calendar have emerged: summer school, the extended school year,[a] and the year-round school.

---

[a]Some YRS literature uses this term as a synonym for year-round school.

1

Summer school is a program during part of or all the summer months that offers students remedial or accelerated work. Summer school can be mandatory or voluntary. The full range of regular school term courses is not offered. Summer schools have existed in many forms for over a century. Some have been described in YRS literature as one quarter of a four-quarter YRS program.

The extended school year is an effort to increase the educational offerings to children by lengthening the amount of time each year that they attend school. For instance, the school term may run from August to July rather than from September to May. This exception to the traditional calendar has been used almost exclusively to increase the educational achievement of students.

Year-round school (YRS) is a system whereby some percentage of students are in attendance in regular terms during each season of the year. Their entry into a new term is staggered throughout the year. What differentiates YRS from other extended programs is the staggered entry of the total student body into the educational cycle; we use the term YRS exclusively in this sense. Unlike the two categories above, these programs have been mounted in the past more for economic (increased plant utilization) than for educational reasons.

## A History of Year-Round Schools

American society in the 1800s was primarily agrarian and consequently most schools operated within the framework of an agrarian economy. Children were needed on the farm from planting to harvest time and therefore schools in agricultural areas were closed from spring until mid-fall.

In the urban areas of the 1800s children were not needed to help with farm work, and therefore many schools operated all year. Evidence exists that Chicago, Boston, Washington, D.C., Cleveland, Buffalo, and Detroit all maintained school sessions of 48 weeks or more.[1] The most popular school schedule of this time was known as the "12-1" plan. It divided the school year up into twelve-week terms with one-week vacations between each term. A modification of this, the "12-4" plan, closed the school for four weeks in August and ran consecutive twelve-week sessions the rest of the year.[2] These types of quarter plans predominated among urban, nineteenth-century schools.

Just after the Civil War there was a trend in urban areas toward the formation of summer schools or vacation schools, an outgrowth of the social reform movement occurring at the time. The first recorded summer school was sponsored in 1865 by the First Church of Boston, Massachusetts. In 1894, the Association for Improving the Conditions of the Poor established summer schools in New York City. Once these early experiments proved successful, public boards of education began making plans for running summer schools of their own. New York instituted a summer session in 1897. Chicago and Providence school systems began summer sessions in 1900. By the turn of the century, summer programs had begun in twenty urban areas. Whereas the purpose of early "vacation schools" was to keep children occupied, the focus later changed from the recreational to the academic and vocational. The typical vacation school of 1910 offered such courses as shoe-making, chair caning, and nursing.[3] According to the U.S. Bureau of Education, by 1916, 200 elementary schools provided one- to three-month summer schools.

In 1912, Newark, New Jersey, began an educational program that, although frequently labeled a year-round school, was actually a summer school program, since the fourth and optional quarter occurred in the summer. The purpose of Newark's summer school was to assimilate its large immigrant population by giving them the additional schooling and English lessons they needed. However, the goals of the program were not realized. The June to August quarter, while considered remediation, actually provided credit for one-third of a year's work. As a result, immigrant students accelerated by attending summer school, and many of them graduated at an early age, inadequately prepared or too immature either to pursue additional education or to enter the labor market.[4]

By World War I, the nine-month school year had become the norm. Table 1-1 indicates how the official school year contracted in urban areas in the seventy-five years between 1840 and 1915.

The standard nine-month calendar of the twentieth century, with its three-month vacation, evolved as a compromise between the needs of the agrarian sector of society for children to be available for farm work and the longer school year of the urban sector. This compromise was engendered by the incorporation of urban and rural areas into school districts. Although this standardization began to occur in the early 1900s, rural and urban areas continued to have incompatible schedules into the 1940s.[5]

After World War I, the combination of an influx of families into

**Table 1-1**
**Length of School Year**

| | Days | |
|---|---|---|
| | *1840* | *1915* |
| Chicago | 240 | 193 |
| Buffalo | 260 | 190 |
| Cleveland | 215 | 192 |
| Detroit | 259 | 191 |
| Philadelphia | 251 | 195 |

industrializing areas and increased birth rates caused enrollments in school districts to expand. During this period, inflating construction costs made many communities reluctant to build additional school facilities. As a result, many communities seriously considered the possibilities of rescheduling the school year.

From the available literature it is not possible to determine whether the school reschedulings that occurred at this time were indeed YRS programs or actually extended summer schools, but some sort of adjustments to the school calendar did occur. Glinke states that the more than 3,000 letters he sent to various school districts requesting information about historical attempts at year-round education revealed a profound lack of information about past experiments. Generally they appear to have been four-quarter programs, and evidence indicates that these programs existed in locations throughout the United States, including Minnesota, Tennessee, Oklahoma, Iowa, and New York.[6]

With the advent of the Great Depression, problems of over-crowding ceased to be acute, and interest in YRS waned. The problem was now one of cutting back programs to save funds. Many YRS programs were discontinued.

During the 1940s and early 1950s, summer school growth was steady if unspectacular. There was strong support for traditional school programs with the school year hovering around the 180-day mark. By 1950, 80 percent of school districts in cities of over 100,000 population had summer programs of some form. Generally, financial support for summer school was provided by state and federal sources, although some funds were provided by local school districts.[7]

In the 1950s, the revival of interest in year-round education was similar to the interest during the post-World War I period. Essentially, it was a response to another crisis: an acute teacher shortage coupled with an escalating student population. Several feasibility studies were performed during this time to explore the four-quarter plan again. A 1951 study in Royal Oak, Michigan, found that while 70 percent of the families returning the questionnaire approved of a twelve-month school operation, 90 percent wanted their children to have vacation in the summer.[8]

A feasibility study in San Mateo County (1951) compared alternatives including double sessions and other variations of staggered all-year plans. The study considered plant utilization, cost effectiveness, and educational results. The study committee was unable to determine clearly the relative advantages of the four-quarter system over the double session plan. However, it concluded that the quarter system would be most advantageous at the high school level, but only if strong community support was enlisted for the plan.[9]

Another feasibility study, conducted by the Los Angeles Board of Education in 1954, concluded that the kinds of curricular changes necessary, combined with the upheaval that would occur in the community, outweighed the potential financial savings of a staggered program. As Dr. Ellis Jarvis, Superintendent of Schools in Los Angeles, stated:

Having had considerable experience with the complexities of setting a calendar for the school year, I am convinced that the 12-month school year can only be established on a large regional or state basis. I say this because of the many interlocking concerns; parents, community groups, institutions of higher education, and the prevailing legal framework for school support.[10]

From 1955 to 1960, some seventeen communities mounted feasibility studies dealing not only with the four-quarter plan but with other plans as well. Fairfield, Connecticut examined the possibility of an eleven-month school year with students attending four hours each day but rejected the plan because it was felt that the social and administrative disadvantages outweighed the advantages.[11] Houston studied a trimester system and planned for its implementation at a later date. Montgomery County, Alabama, and DeKalb and Fulton Counties in Georgia studied the staggered four-quarter system. The communities that conducted these studies represented a geographic cross section of the United States as well as an assortment of urban, rural, and suburban communities.

From 1962 to 1967, the Florida State University laboratory school developed a trimester plan. The pilot study consisted of three seventy-five-day terms with students from grades 1-12. Classes were nongraded, both organizationally and educationally. The study was terminated in 1967.

In 1963, Nova High School in Ft. Lauderdale, Florida, developed a 220-day school year plan. Classes were graded, but individual progression was encouraged. Under the Nova plan, movement from tenth grade to graduation could be accomplished in 2.3 years. Initially, this plan had the full support of the local community, particularly of students and parents. However, it was discontinued in 1965 because of strain on students and teachers caused by the lack of an extended vacation from Easter to the end of July. Students showed a psychological letdown from being in school for seven weeks longer than students in nearby schools. Family vacation schedules were inconvenienced, and the school administration had difficulties with the school budget and teacher certification.

While the trimester was not a widely studied or implemented extended school year plan, San Jacinto High School in Houston piloted a trimester plan in 1968. Students were allowed to attend two of three terms and were allowed to pay to attend school for any additional time exceeding the 175-day tuition-free school year.[1][2]

In the mid-1960s, New York State carried out major studies to determine the effect of an extended school year on parents, teachers, students, and school district finances. The programs included:

1. Commack's Continuous Progress Plan. In 1964, one Commack elementary school adopted an eleven-month school year. In August, 1967, the program was considered successful enough to be expanded to four elementary schools.

2. Cato-Meridian's Quadrimester Plan. In 1964, a modified elementary school quadrimester program was instituted in grades K to 6 of a central school. A combination of a lengthened school day plus a small extension of the school year provided the equivalent of a weighted school year of approximately 220 to 225 school days.

3. Syosset's Modified Summer School Program for Junior High School. An experimental group of seventh grade students worked through three modified summer school programs to demonstrate the feasibility of taking first time, full-year courses in six weeks.

4. Hornell's Modified Summer Segment for Secondary School Students. Junior and senior high school students took first time, full-year courses in seven weeks of summer activity to demonstrate the feasibility of teaching and learning in compacted time blocks.[13]

In Commac, at the Grace Hubbs Elementary School, a "continuous progress extended school year" with 200 grade 1-4 students was attempted. The school term ran from August to July (210 days). Findings were that students scored higher on standardized achievement tests and had a high attendance rate in the summer. Parental reaction was quite positive to this program.

The Cato-Meridian Central School developed and operated a modified quadrimester in 1964-1967. The school year was 200 days, actually the equivalent of 220 regular school days since each day was approximately forty-nine minutes longer than a standard day. The program was strongly resisted by parents, teachers, and students. Although the school schedule was staggered, with not all students attending all 200 days of classes, most people viewed the plan as a disruption of personal schedules.

While school districts during this period began to experiment with rescheduling the school year as a means of revising the curriculum, such plans did not achieve widespread popularity or success. People continued to resist a rescheduled school year because too frequently it disrupted the vacation and life-style of the family.

Not until 1968, with the development and implementation of the 45-15 plan in Valley View, Illinois, did YRS begin to achieve the broad-based support it has at present. In 1953, the district had eighty-five pupils. By 1969, the number of students had grown to 5000, and the district was faced with enrolling an additional 1700 in the 1970-1971 school year. During the 1960s, the Valley View taxpayers had supported construction of seven new school buildings. However, the state directed that, by 1970, each elementary school district must provide a kindergarten program, thereby further straining the district's resources. Hence the district developed a 45-15 plan for the total school district, the first of its kind in the country, after an analysis of rescheduled school calendars of the past seventy years. In theory and practice, only 75 percent of the student body is in attendance at any one time in the school year. The school plant operates the year round; students in each of four groups attend school for forty-five days and are off for fifteen days. Efforts are made to include children from one family and neighborhood in the same attendance group. Valley View tried this alternative primarily to avoid the additional tax burden of building new facilities to service the increasing student population in particular the new kindergarten students.

The development of 45-15 achieved three major innovations that overcame the drawbacks of earlier YRS plans and contributed significantly to the growth and popularity of YRS today. The 45-15 plan provided: a summer vacation for all children; a rescheduled school year that does not necessarily accelerate students out of a school system at too early an age; and a series of shorter and more frequent vacations than the traditional school schedule.

The 45-15 plan and subsequent revised school schedules had an important effect on people's attitudes toward YRS: they made YRS more acceptable. School districts began to realize that YRS had an inherent value. While most YRS programs continued to be implemented out of necessity as responses to fiscal crisis and overcrowding, YRS began to achieve legitimacy as a desirable and even preferable school schedule. Districts that did not need to revise their schedules began to do so anyway, and districts that were forced to implement a YRS plan discovered the plan's curricular benefits. Districts also began to reconsider the values of some of the earlier YRS plans tried in the 1950s and 1960s; many of these were implemented successfully.

For example, in 1968, Atlanta instituted a four-quarter plan at the high school level aimed at greater flexibility and responsiveness to individual student needs. This plan was developed in view of the perceived wide range of life-styles and changing needs of the many communities and individuals within Atlanta, and it continues today. Students are allowed to develop their own schedules and may combine work with school, accelerate, remediate, or attend a traditional school program. Courses have been structured so that students progress through the school system at their own pace. This means they may attend all four quarters or fractions of quarters, just so long as they satisfy the state's requirements regarding minimum annual or daily hours of instruction.

Atlanta was one of the first school systems to begin a YRS program out of belief in its relevance to the needs of the day. The cultural upheavals of the late 1960s and early 1970s caused other school districts to look toward YRS for the same reasons.

In 1969, the first national conference on year-round schools was held in Fayetteville, Arkansas. By 1974, nineteen states had rewritten old laws and regulations to incorporate year-round education programs into their statutes. By this time there were approximately 100 operational YRS programs in the country; an additional ninety-six districts were either conducting feasibility studies or planning or implementing some form of YRS or extended school year program.

These figures on the prevalence of YRS differ from those shown in a survey of state education agencies conducted by the New Jersey Department of Education in 1975.[14] Ours is a narrower definition than that used in the survey. For instance, sixty-one districts in Georgia tallied as operating YRS programs in the 1975 survey organize their curricula by quarters, but attendance in the quarters is not staggered nor are the summer quarters tuition-free. Therefore, these sixty-one districts do not by our definition offer YRS programs.

To summarize this history, communities turned to YRS when they were faced with an influx of new students (as at the end of both World Wars, or during periods of heavy immigration), a teacher shortage, or when they wished to maximize existing school facilities while postponing the building of new facilities. Only in recent times (Atlanta's reorganization of its entire curriculum is the major example) have school systems viewed year-round schools as a means of upgrading the quality of the curriculum.

### Currently Operating Varieties of Year-Round Schools

YRS is simply a way of organizing school attendance so that some of the students are in school at any time of the year while the remainder are on vacation. This principle can take a variety of forms, however, when it is actually put into practice. This variety is one of the advantages YRS offers. Communities can design the school calendar that best fits their needs. Although the traditional school calendar is nearly universal, there is no a priori reason to believe that any particular school calendar is best for all communities. Debate about YRS, for whatever reason it is initiated, allows the community to consider various ways of organizing the school calendar and to select the one which suits it best.

The six YRS plans described below are not a complete catalog; rather, they are basic types that encompass most other variations.

Once the differences between these basic types are understood, a school planning a YRS program can select and modify the type that best meets its needs. Figure 1-1 shows the distribution of different types of YRS programs in 1975.

It should be stressed that educational innovations do not necessarily occur simply because the school year is rescheduled. The new school schedule should be accompanied by planning and redesign of the curriculum and teacher training. Otherwise even the most innovative and flexible school schedule will not automatically lead to educational gains.

These YRS programs may have either mandated or voluntary schedules. In the first instance, the school district assigns students to a particular combination of school terms and vacations. As will be shown in Chapter 2, mandated programs are common in districts that have turned to YRS for economic reasons. If economy and space savings are not of primary importance or are not immediately critical, a YRS program may be voluntary. In this case, students are either allowed to decide what terms they will attend in a school year or whether they will attend a year-round or a traditional school in the system.

Depending on the plan in effect, year-round schools are in session from 220 days to 258 days per year. Individual students usually do not attend school for more than 175 to 180 days a year (a major difference from the nineteenth-century programs). At any given time, from 20 percent to 33 percent of the students are on vacation, depending on the plan used. In contrast, schools using a traditional calendar (see Figure 1-2) are open for about 180 days a year; all students attend at the same time and are on summer vacation at the same time.

*The 45-15 School Year*

As can be seen from Figure 1-1, the 45-15 plan is currently the most popular YRS model. Under this plan, students are divided into four equal groups. Each group attends school for forty-five days and then has a fifteen-day vacation. The groups' schedules are staggered (see Figure 1-3); theoretically, the school can accommodate 33 percent more students than would be possible if it were on a traditional calendar. However, the fifteen-day vacation periods can optionally be used for enrichment, remediation, or acceleration. In this case, somewhat less than 25 percent of the students would be on vacation at any given time.

The 45-15 plan may also have educational benefits; it has been hypothesized that students forget less over short three-week vacations and that therefore teachers can cover more new material each new forty-five-day period. The plan is more popular at the primary than at the secondary level. Given the usual wide array of courses in high school, the frequent opening and closing of instructional periods places a great strain on scheduling, registration, and testing processes and probably increases costs. Also, 45-15 does not easily lend itself to a combination of work and study throughout the school year, and the series of short vacations make it difficult for high school students to find a job during those periods.

To minimize disruption, children from the same families and same general neighborhood are usually placed in the same session and calendars can be worked out a year or more in advance so families can plan activities accordingly.

Typically, the curriculum is redesigned so that instruction is flexibly packaged in forty-five day segments. If it is desirable for children to repeat work for the purpose of strengthening basic skills, they may enroll in the next forty-five-day session that covers the same learning experiences.

Under the 45-15 plan, several employment options are available to teachers. For instance, a teacher may work forty-five days on and fifteen days off. In this situation, the teacher can remain with the same group of students throughout the year and teach no more than the traditional 180 days. At the other end of the continuum, a teacher may take on a new group of students each forty-five days and work throughout the 240-day school year. Salaries are usually increased correspondingly.

*The Four-Quarter School Year*

Of the YRS models in use today, the four-quarter plan (see Figure 1-4) is the oldest and most familiar. Although earlier it was used primarily for remediation or for acceleration (in order to reduce overcrowding), it is now used most frequently for curriculum innovation, as in Atlanta, Georgia. Where economy is also an

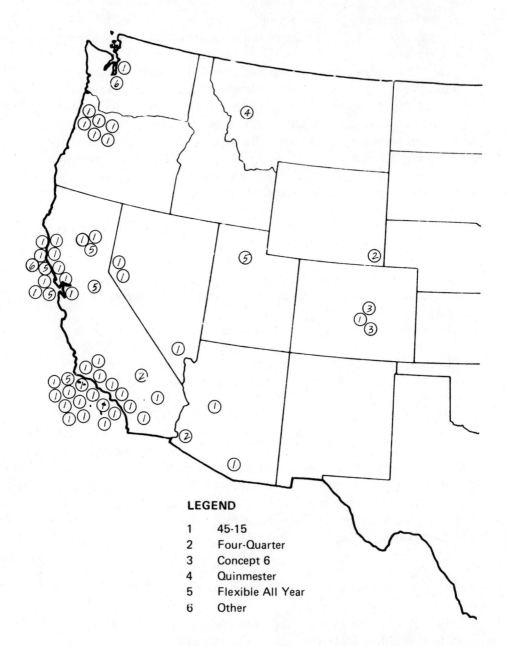

**LEGEND**

| | |
|---|---|
| 1 | 45-15 |
| 2 | Four-Quarter |
| 3 | Concept 6 |
| 4 | Quinmester |
| 5 | Flexible All Year |
| 6 | Other |

Source: Year-Round Education Activities in the United States, Trenton, N.J.: New Jersey Department of Education, 1975.

**Figure 1-1.** Year-Round School Programs, by Model, 1975.

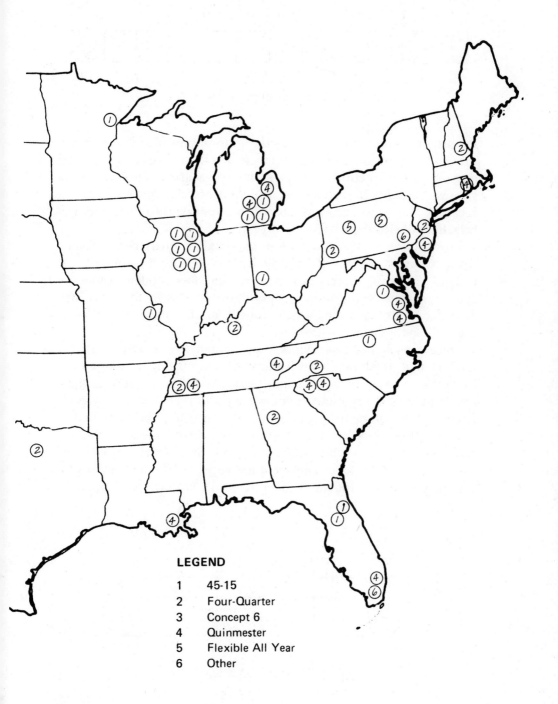

**LEGEND**

| | |
|---|---|
| 1 | 45-15 |
| 2 | Four-Quarter |
| 3 | Concept 6 |
| 4 | Quinmester |
| 5 | Flexible All Year |
| 6 | Other |

14

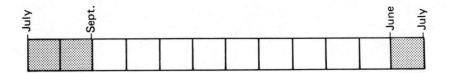

**Figure 1-2.** The Traditional School Year.

important factor, attendance on the four-quarter plan is mandated; the students are divided into four equal groups and assigned three quarters of instruction and a quarter of vacation. To achieve the greatest savings, 25 percent of the students should always be on vacation. The theoretical savings will be equivalent to those that can be achieved with the 45-15 school year.

Instruction is planned within the flexible quarter-year framework. Courses can be of varying lengths to suit the content; for instance, in-depth courses can span two quarters. Students can enter and leave courses at various points during the year. Students may even accelerate by attending the fourth quarter; however, if that is the case, space savings will be lost.

One reason for this school year's popularity at the secondary level is that it allows for a variety of work/study combinations. Students on vacation should find it easier to locate a job, since there are 75 percent fewer students competing with them for employment. Alternatively, students planning their own schedules may find it feasible to combine work with study on a daily basis if they spend less time per day in class and spread class attendance out over the four quarters. Such an arrangement has very positive implications for the disadvantaged student who must work, but who would like to

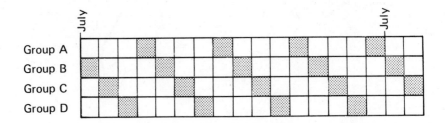

**Figure 1-3.** The 45-15 School Year.

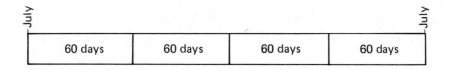

**Figure 1-4.** The Four-Quarter School Year.

finish high school or go to college. As it is, such students often find that economic realities frustrate their desire for further education.

The timing of vacations under a mandated four-quarter plan may disrupt family vacation schedules; school districts must be prepared to deal with this problem.

*The Concept 6 School Year*

Concept 6 is a very new model, developed as an alternative to 45-15. As the term Concept 6 implies, the school year is divided into six terms of instruction; each consists of approximately forty-three days. Students must attend four of the six terms. Depending on the degree of need to economize, a fifth term may also be available to students on an optional basis.

When economizing is essential, students are divided into three equal groups, and school and vacation periods are staggered, as shown in Figure 1-5. Potentially, a school mandating this plan can accommodate 50 percent more students than it could under the traditional calendar year. Facilities are also used more intensively— the Concept 6 school year is 258 days long.

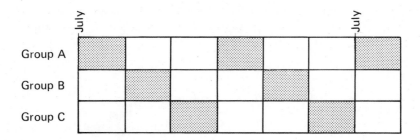

**Figure 1-5.** The Concept 6 School Year.

Among its other advantages, Concept 6 allows for a more traditional vacation pattern. All students have two seasonal vacations—one in warm weather and one in cool weather. Concept 6 also eliminates the frequent scheduling and grade recording of 45-15. It is, therefore, a more feasible model for secondary schools and provides two opportunities for work experience in a school year.

*The Quinmester School Year*

In the Quinmester model, the school year is divided into five forty-five-day quins; students must attend four. With 20 percent of the student body on vacation at any one time, a school can make do with 25 percent less space than it would otherwise need. If economic pressures are not strong, students can attend a fifth quin. (See Figure 1-6.)

Dividing a year into a series of forty-five-day quins provides opportunities for developing shorter, more intense courses than are possible with the traditional calendar—an option particularly attractive at the high school level. Full academic offerings are available in each quin. This allows great flexibility to pupils in their curricular choices. The usual problems with family vacations may occur.

*The Trimester School Year*

The YRS model that seems to be the least popular is the Trimester. As Figure 1-7 shows, the school year is divided into three terms of approximately seventy-five days apiece. (A small increase in the length of each school day is necessary to meet state minimum standards.) Students must attend two of the three terms; attendance patterns may be either mandated and staggered or voluntary, in

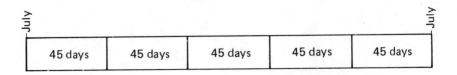

**Figure 1-6.** The Quinmester School Year.

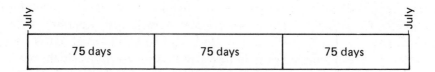

**Figure 1-7.** The Trimester School Year.

which case the third term may be available to students. Of course, if a district wishes to achieve the plan's potentially great savings, it should guarantee that one-third of the total student population is always on vacation.

*The Flexible Year-Round School Year*

Some school districts use year-round schools to achieve ultimate flexibility in calendar and curriculum. These districts have developed models that maximize a school's responsiveness to each student, even though costs may rise.

The flexible year-round model represented in Figure 1-8 does not impose arbitrary blocks of time, such as quins or quarters, on the school year. The school operates about fifty weeks a year; attendance patterns and vacation schedules are left entirely up to the discretion of the student, so long as the state minimum requirements are met. Students are actually encouraged to attend more than the minimum number of days. The curriculum is totally restructured to facilitate continuous progress on an individualized basis.

Such a plan permits students to begin the school year at any point and to select courses, attendance patterns, and vacations as their needs dictate. Course lengths vary, and students progress at their own pace. Students may select a traditional calendar, a

**Figure 1-8.** The Flexible Year-Round School Year.

shortened calendar, or an extended calendar. Options are generally available for enrichment, remediation, or acceleration experiences.

Some schools may find that the totally flexible calendar is too difficult to implement, as it requires the complete individualization of the curriculum. If a school is attracted to the advantages of a flexible calendar but wants a program divided into blocks of time, programs such as those illustrated in Figures 1-9 and 1-10 may fill their needs.

In the first alternative, students attend any twelve of the sixteen time blocks. Each block represents fifteen days. The number of students on vacation at any one time may vary.

The second alternative features overlapping periods of forty-five days in length. A student attends school during any four nonoverlapping time segments (e.g., lines 1, 4, 9, and 12). Again, the number of students on vacation at any one time may vary.

### Conclusions

As the three examples of the flexible year-round calendar illustrate, none of the ways of scheduling school attendance presented above is hard and fast. Using one of these six frameworks, a community should be able to develop a school calendar uniquely tailored to its special needs. One can speculate that if there is a wave of the future in YRS, it is the flexible calendar. However, its advantages depend on such long-run social trends as changing life-styles; for most schools, immediate and pressing economic concerns make the 45-15, Concept 6, or Quinmester plans more attractive. Chapter 2 describes school districts that have considered one or another of these basic varieties of YRS.

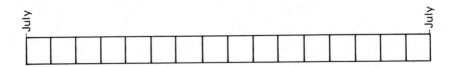

**Figure 1-9.** Separate Blocked Flexible Year-Round School Year.

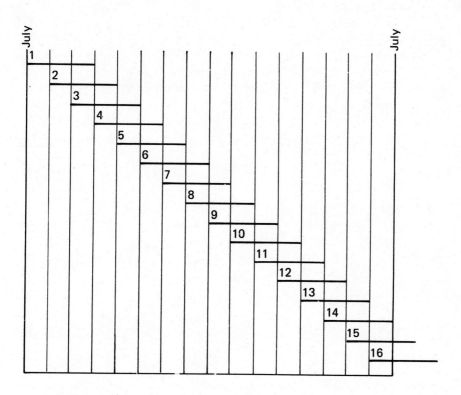

**Figure 1-10.** Overlapping Blocked Flexible Year-Round School Year.

# 2

## The Current State of Year-Round Schools

Year-round school programs thrive in some school districts and wither away in others. This chapter begins with case studies of three districts that have had different experiences with YRS. It then presents the results of a systematic analysis of such programs in twenty-four school districts (the first systematic analysis of operative YRS programs ever conducted). Finally, an entire state's experience with YRS is described. What emerges is a picture of the ways that YRS programs actually operate and the impacts they have on their communities.

### Case Studies

Some school districts have implemented YRS programs; others have decided not to; still others, once embarked on YRS, have abandoned it. Consider the experience of Chino, a suburban California community. Its 57,000 people are mostly white, with a strong admixture of Spanish-speakers. Chino's residents represent a wide variety of socioeconomic levels.

In the early 1970s Chino began to experience rapid growth. The land that was once largely dairy farms began to be divided up into suburban tracts when former residents of Los Angeles moved out toward the north. As many of Chino's dairy farms were subdivided, a significant number of the Mexican-American migrants who had worked these farms took jobs in industry in the area and became permanent residents of Chino.

The district's student population expanded. School administrators recognized that more efficient use would have to be made of school facilities, especially at the elementary levels. Administrators therefore investigated the possibilities of 45-15, which had already been successfully implemented in a number of California elementary schools. A feasibility study was conducted, and the public was surveyed to determine its reactions to such a plan. In support of its preparations for YRS, Chino received both financial and technical assistance from California.

Chino decided to implement a voluntary 45-15 program in two elementary schools housing grades K-8 beginning with the 1973-1974 school year. Once this decision was made, teacher training sessions were held, curricula revised, teacher contracts negotiated or adjustments made, a public relations effort launched, and additional surveys conducted of community attitudes toward the model. The citizens were not directly involved in Chino's planning activities, but they were kept informed about the program through various means, including PTA meetings. Initially, only 1300 students were involved, but the year following initial implementation 45-15 was expanded to seven additional elementary schools and to grade nine in the high school. This expansion raised the total number of students involved to 7600.

Overall, Chino's YRS program is viewed very positively by district residents. However, those who prefer their children to attend a traditional school program have raised strong objections to YRS. The children who want a traditional program are generally bused out of their neighborhoods, and the busing upsets their parents.

YRS has alleviated Chino's space problem at present. If another student population boom develops, Chino plans expansion of YRS to additional schools. Teachers and students both find the new school schedule to be more stimulating and see advantages in the new curriculum.

The YRS experience was different in the Champlain Valley Union High School District, which serves five suburban-rural Vermont communities near Lake Champlain. In the face of a rapidly growing enrollment due to the expanding of new industries in the district, an additional high school was proposed. In 1968 the voters failed to pass a bond issue for the school, and the Board of Education formed an Ad Hoc Committee to look into alternative ways of handling the space problem.

This Committee, in reviewing YRS literature, came across the 45-15 plan. Attracted to it not only because it was a potential space saver, but also because it had possibilities for curriculum innovation, the Committee studied the 45-15 plan in depth. The Board stipulated that the Committee had to keep the public informed while studying and then planning for 45-15. This schedule had already been implemented in several elementary districts in the United States, though not at the high school level. Consequently many of the problems and details unique to 45-15 at the high school level had neither been identified nor worked out at the time the Committee began its study.

As the Committee "felt its way" through the planning of 45-15 while simultaneously informing the public of its actions and progress, the public began to view the Committee's activities and decisions as unsystematic and disorganized. The Committee, on the other hand, perceived its progress as orderly and logical in view of the new ground it was breaking in YRS.

Coupled with the residents' growing dissatisfaction with the Committee's activities was the Committee and Board's misinterpretation of the public's basic attitude toward the plan. Despite a series of open meetings and a nonbinding referendum to measure opinion toward YRS, the public's unhappiness with the way in which 45-15 was being planned for did not register clearly with the Board. Consequently, when the Board announced plans to implement 45-15, the community became embroiled in heated controversy over the way the Board had handled the study of YRS. As a result, the next year the Board rescinded its decision.

Interest in YRS continued, however, and new committees were formed to study YRS, this time including not just representatives from the administration and School Board but also representatives from the high school faculty, students, and community. Working together they determined exactly what sorts of opportunities they would like their high school to provide students and what school schedule would best fit these goals. What resulted was the development of the Multiple Access Plan, which divides the year into fifteen nine-week terms. Students are required to attend four of these terms in any combination they desire. A fifth term is available as an option. Such schedule flexibility and the innovative curriculum developed by the teachers allowed students within the Multiple Access Plan to attend on a traditional schedule, an accelerated schedule, or a wide variety of individualized schedules.

The Multiple Access Plan was implemented in the fall of 1972. Despite its promise as an ultimately flexible, innovative schedule, it lasted only about a year. The plan was discontinued, because, although residents wished to have a nontraditional schedule available to students and although an array of outdoor activities is available throughout the year in the areas, most students simply did not choose to attend school on a nontraditional schedule. In essence, the very nature of the Multiple Access Plan—an innovative, flexible, nonmandated program—worked against the most pressing goal of YRS in this district, to use the school facility most efficiently. Multiple Access made it too easy for students to continue attending school in the way they were used to, i.e., the traditional school schedule.

Elk Grove, California is a community located about ten miles down the freeway from Sacramento. About a decade ago it was largely farmland but because of its proximity to an urban center its open spaces began to disappear as developers purchased the land and built homes on it. As Elk Grove became suburban, the school-aged population swelled beyond the capacity of its schools.

This problem became especially acute in Elk Grove's single high school. District administrators, in searching out ways to handle overcrowding in the high school, decided to investigate the possibilities of YRS. In 1970, a Year-Round School Study Committee reviewed various YRS models and recommended that 45-15 be studied further. A second committee was subsequently set up to include interested citizens in the study of 45-15.

The study Elk Grove conducted of the feasibility of 45-15 at the high school level stands apart from most other districts' efforts as being very well planned and complete. An explanation for the quality of the study may be that Elk Grove received an ESEA Title III grant to be applied toward its study of YRS as well as technical assistance from the State Department of Education.

Elements of Elk Grove's 45-15 feasibility study included:

needs assessment and goal setting

economic feasibility study

development of a computer program capable of creating a master schedule for 45-15

preparation and distribution of districtwide opinion survey

curriculum revision and development of instructional aids

development of appropriate management and accounting procedures

staff training and orientation

dissemination of information to public through preparation of newsletters and new releases.

Despite the breadth of activities conducted by Elk Grove in its feasibility study and its attempts to include citizens in the study and keep the general public informed, negative public opinion defeated YRS in this district.

The mismanagement of the public relations effort appears to have been the downfall of YRS here. Rather than stressing the inherent desirability of YRS as a way of making the curriculum more exciting and relevant to students, district administrators approached the subject in much the same fashion as had administrators of YRS programs in the past. They tried to portray YRS as a temporary measure to be continued until a new high school was built. Because this approach did not clearly define for citizens the educational values of YRS, and because they were willing to pay for a new high school, citizen reaction to the study was generally that it was a waste of time and effort. Double shifts or extended days seemed to them to be a more reasonable temporary solution.

Citizens perceived a dichotomy between what the administrators said YRS was to accomplish and the effort expended on its study, especially in view of public willingness to allow double or extended sessions until the new high school was built. They concluded that the feasibility study was in fact "window dressing" for a decision already made—to implement 45-15. Discontent grew as opponents pointed out that the mandatory nature of the proposed plan for Elk Grove's only high school reduced attendance options for students; also, with high schoolers assigned to one schedule and grade schoolers to another, traditional, schedule, it was possible that families with children of both ages would not be able to take vacations together. Backers of Elk Grove's very successful athletics program feared its destruction by YRS, while the small farm community that remained in Elk Grove decried the loss of farm labor that they felt 45-15 would cause.

When a vote was finally taken, the margin was 4 to 3 in favor of not implementing YRS. While the mechanics of planning had been well executed, the sensitive and crucial area of public relations had been poorly dealt with. In the end, emotionalism based on a misunderstanding of the potential of YRS defeated it in Elk Grove.

## Demographic and Programmatic Data

This section first sketches certain demographic characteristics of twenty-four school districts across the nation that have been involved with YRS. The ensuing comparison of the districts' programs suggests the variety of plans and of activities that comprises the YRS movement today.

As can be seen from Table 2-1, districts involved range in population from 7500 (Mora, Minnesota) to 1,000,000 (Dade County, Florida). YRS is primarily a suburban phenomenon, although it is also occurring in urban and rural districts. The residents of districts with YRS programs are employed in a wide range of occupations. Although nearly every district studied, except the most urban, termed itself middle class, occupational data indicate that some districts are primarily blue-collar working class (Valley View, Illinois) and that others are heavily professional (La Mesa-Spring Valley and Hayward, California). Several districts indicated that they have a sizeable military population (Virginia Beach, Virginia, and Colorado Springs, Colorado). The populations of the rural districts generally comprise small farm owners, a scattering of professionals, and blue-collar workers.

The difficulty encountered in obtaining consistent data prevents a systematic analysis of ethnic makeup by total school district population, but it is safe to say that all the districts except Atlanta and Dade County are predominantly white. Atlanta, Georgia has a large black population; Dade County, Florida has a sizeable number of black and Spanish-speaking residents. Many of the Spanish-speakers in YRS districts are Mexican-Americans residing in California.

It has been hypothesized that YRS, in particular the 45-15 plan, serves a compensatory education function for disadvantaged children. However, data were not often available regarding how many disadvantaged children are in a school district and what percentage of these are in YRS programs.

Among the districts studied, YRS is most frequently implemented at the elementary level, generally using the 45-15 model (see Table 2-2). Of the twenty-four districts, twenty-one studied and implemented 45-15. All but five of these twenty-one districts began their programs at the elementary or elementary to junior high level. Milpitas, California began 45-15 districtwide, but the scheduling problems the program created at the high school level were one of the reasons it was discontinued. All three of those districts that studied but did not implement YRS were considering 45-15.

Of the six districts that did not choose 45-15, one elementary school implemented a four-quarter plan, another the Concept 6 plan. Dade County, which began its YRS for all grades, implemented a quinmester plan. Atlanta, Georgia; Hudson, New Hampshire; and Champlain Valley, Vermont began their YRS programs at the high school level. Atlanta and Hudson both began four-quarter plans, while Champlain Valley implemented a Multiple Access plan.

About one-half of the districts studied that actually implemented YRS expanded their programs over time. As the community grew to accept and understand YRS and as YRS demonstrated its effectiveness as a means to save space and money or to introduce educational innovations, YRS programs were either expanded to additional grade levels or to other schools in the district (see Table 2-3). Seven districts expanded both the grade levels and the total number of schools involved in a year-round school program. One of these seven districts expanded its program districtwide, and three expanded the total number of schools involved. Eleven experienced no expansion at all; none of the discontinued programs expanded. Atlanta actually decreased the total size of its program by both number of schools and number of children because of a lack of state financial aid and the high cost of running the program.

Atlanta's YRS program has not only been drastically reduced in scope and size, but its very existence is threatened by the lack of interest and cooperation it receives from the Georgia state government. This threat to Atlanta's program points up what may be a contributing factor either to the failure or to the success and growth of YRS—the attitude of state governments toward YRS (see Table 2-4). If a state does not at least recognize the existence of YRS programs and make special provisions for them, the programs appear to have great difficulty in acquiring state aid and reimbursements during those times of the year when they are operating but traditional schools are not.

For example, the Francis Howell school district in Missouri has experienced great difficulty due to its location in a state where no enabling legislation exists for YRS. Francis Howell implemented YRS as the most feasible answer to its severe overcrowding problems. Conversations with individuals in the district indicate that the

**Table 2-1**
**Demographic Data for Twenty-four School Districts**

| | Total Population | Community Type | | | Ethnic Breakdown (percent) | | | | | Occupational Characteristics | | | | | | |
|---|---|---|---|---|---|---|---|---|---|---|---|---|---|---|---|---|
| | | Urban | Suburban | Rural | Black | Spanish-Speaking | American Indian | White | Other | Professional | Blue Collar | Agricultural | Migrant | Military | Tourist-related | Broad Spectrum |
| **Successful** | | | | | | | | | | | | | | | | |
| Hesperia, Ca. | 10.5 | | | x | <1 | | | 99 | | x | x | x | | x | | |
| Chino, Ca. | 57.0 | | x | | <1 | 27 | <1 | 68 | | x | x | | | | | x |
| Corona Norco, Ca. | 74.0 | | x | | <1 | 25 | | 75 | | x | x | | | x | | x |
| Chula Vista, Ca. | 110.0 | | x | | 10 | 20 | | 65 | 5 | x | x | | | | | |
| Hayward, Ca. | 24.0 | | x | | 4.5 | 19.2 | <1 | 74 | 3.9 | x | x | | | | | |
| La Mesa-Spring Valley, Ca. | 75.0 | | x | | <1 | 10 | | 90 | | x | x | | | | | |
| Pajaro Valley, Ca. | 90.0 | | | x | <1 | 50 | | 50 | | x | x | x | x | | | |
| Colorado Springs, Co. | 200.0 | x | | | 6 | 9 | 0.3 | 84 | 0.8 | x | x | | | x | x | |
| Molalla, Or. | 7.5 | | x | x | <1 | | <1 | 99 | <1 | x | x | x | | | | |
| Mora, Mn. | 16.0 | | | x | <1 | | <1 | 99 | <1 | x | x | x | | | | |
| Francis Howell, Mo. | 18.0 | | x | x | <1 | <1 | | 99 | <1 | x | x | x | | | | |
| Northville, Mi. | 42.0 | | x | | <1 | | | 99 | | x | x | | | | | |
| Valley View, Il. | | | x | x | 5 | 7.5 | | 85 | | x | x | | | | | |
| Prince William County, Va. | 160.0 | | x | | 7 | 1 | | 92 | | x | x | | | | | |
| Atlanta, Ga. | 500.0 | x | | | 88 | <1 | | 10 | <1 | x | | | | | | |
| Dade County, Fl. | 1000.0 | x | x | | 65 | | | 35 | <1 | | | | | | | x |
| Hudson, N.H. | 13.0 | | x | | <1 | | | 99 | | | x | | | | | x |

| | | | | | | | | | | | |
|---|---|---|---|---|---|---|---|---|---|---|---|
| **Discontinued** | | | | | | | | | | | |
| Milpitas, Ca. | 30.0 | x | | 7 | 16 | 77 | | x | | | x |
| Loudoun County, Va. | 42.0 | x | | 12 | <1 | 85 | 1 | x | x | x | x |
| Virginia Beach, Va. | 220.0 | x | | 15 | | 85 | | x | x | x | x |
| Champlain Valley, Vt. | 10.0 | x | x | <1 | | 99 | | x | x | x | x |
| **Not Implemented** | | | | | | | | | | | |
| Elk Grove, Ca. | 40.0 | x | x | 2 | 9 | 85 | 3 | | | | x |
| Roswell, N.M. | 45.0 | x | x | 4 | 31 | 65 | | x | x | x | x |
| Pennebury, Pa. | 52.0 | x | | <1 | <1 | 99 | | x | x | x | x |

[a]Numbers given in thousands.

**Table 2-2**
**Implementation of YRS Programs**

| | Model | Grades Affected at Start of Program |
|---|---|---|
| **Successful** | | |
| Hesperia, Ca. | 45-15 | K-6 |
| Chino, Ca. | 45-15 | K-8 |
| Corona Norco, Ca. | 45-15 | K-9 |
| Chula Vista, Ca. | 45-15 | K-6 |
| Hayward, Ca. | 4 Quarter | K-6 |
| La Mesa-Spring Valley, Ca. | 45-15 | K-8 |
| Pajaro Valley, Ca. | 45-15 | K-8 |
| Colorado Springs, Co. | Concept 6/4 Quarter | K-8 |
| Molalla, Or. | 45-15 | 1-8 |
| Mora, Mn. | 45-15 | 1-6 |
| Francis Howell, Mo. | 45-15 | 1-6 |
| Northville, Mi. | 45-15 | K-5 |
| Valley View, Il. | 45-15 | K-8 |
| Prince William County, Va. | 45-15 | 1-8 |
| Atlanta, Ga. | 4 Quarter | 8-12 |
| Dade County, Fl. | Quinmester | 7-12 |
| Hudson, N.H. | 4 Quarter | 9-12 |
| **Discontinued** | | |
| Milpitas, Ca. | 45-15 | K-12 |
| Loudoun County, Va. | 45-15 | 1-8 |
| Virginia Beach, Va. | 45-15 | K-7 |
| Champlain Valley, Vt. | Multiple Access | 9-12 |
| **Not Implemented** | | |
| Elk Grove, Ca. | 45-15 | |
| Roswell, N.M. | 45-15 | |
| Pennebury, Pa. | 45-15 | |

establishment and continued operation of this program have demanded a constant struggle both to ensure that it receives the state reimbursements to which it is entitled and to counteract the isolation it naturally feels as the only program of its type in the state.

The Molalla, Oregon program has had similar difficulties. While legislation has been passed in that state to allow schools that operate year-round their fair share of state aid, in reality such support has been almost impossible to acquire. Lack of state aid has prevented Molalla from remedying its severe shortage of YRS-related administrative and clerical help.

The situation in these states is in sharp contrast to that in California, where the state government actively promotes YRS and assists districts in the implementation, operation, and evaluation of their programs. (See the California study in the following section.)

Five of the seventeen districts with successful YRS programs indicated that they received federal money to study the feasibility of YRS through Title III of the Elementary and Secondary Education Act (ESEA) of 1965 as did all the districts that studied but did not implement a YRS program (see Table 2-4). Three successful programs indicated that they applied Title I ESEA money to their year-round program. No district appears to have used Title IV funds in connection with YRS.

The twenty-four school districts provided two basic reasons for studying or implementing YRS—economic and educational (see Table 2-5). Nearly half indicated they were motivated to study YRS by overcrowding and financial pressures. Nine districts stated that a combination of these factors and the educational benefits possible in a rescheduled school year motivated them. Only three turned to YRS for its educational benefits alone. Finally, one district in Pajaro Valley, California, which has a very large Mexican-American population, implemented YRS to handle its overcrowding problems and achieve greater ethnic balance in its schools. Evidence indicates that a YRS plan, if implemented properly, can facilitate integration by distributing racial groups of students evenly throughout the terms of the year.

Little relationship can be identified between the types of YRS models implemented by a district and the factors that motivated their implementation. Hence there is no basis for concluding that certain types of models are frequently selected to solve particular types of problems. The lack of relationship probably indicates that the model chosen is determined by such immediate, practical concerns as "Will it work in our district?" or "Will the community, students, and teachers like it?"

As Table 2-5 suggests, a greater causal relationship seems to exist between the reason YRS is implemented and whether a district allows it students to opt in or out of a YRS program. Of the districts that operate or operated YRS programs for space/economic reasons,

Table 2-3
Expansion of YRS Programs

| | # Schools in District | # Schools in YRS at Start of Program | # Schools in YRS after Expansion | # Students in District[a] | # Students Attending YRS Schools at Start of Program[a] | # Students Attending YRS Schools after Expansion[a] | Grades Affected at Start of Program | Grades Affected after Expansion |
|---|---|---|---|---|---|---|---|---|
| Successful | | | | | | | | |
| Hesperia, Ca. | 3 | 3 | N.E.[b] | 1.0 | 1.0 | N.E. | K-6 | N.E. |
| Chino, Ca. | 17 | 2 | 9 | 8.8 | 1.3 | 7.6 | K-8 | K-9 |
| Corona Norco, Ca. | 28 | 4 | 16 | 15.6 | 0.8 | 7.3 | K-9 | K-12 |
| Chula Vista, Ca. | 26 | 4 | 7 | 13.0 | 4.0 | 5.3 | K-6 | K-6 |
| Hayward, Ca. | 34 | 1 | N.E. | 13.0 | 0.4 | N.E. | K-6 | N.E. |
| La Mesa-Spring Valley, Ca. | 22 | 3 | 4 | 15.0 | 2.0 | 2.7 | K-8 | K-8 |
| Pajaro Valley, Ca. | 21 | 5 | N.E. | 13.0 | 2.5 | N.E. | K-8 | N.E. |
| Colorado Springs, Co. | 50 | 2 | 5 | 35.0 | 2.0 | 5.2 | K-8 | K-8 |
| Molalla, Or. | 1 | 1 | N.E. | 1.1 | 1.1 | N.E. | 1-8 | N.E. |
| Mora, Mn. | 4 | 1 | N.E. | 1.9 | 1.0 | N.E. | 1-6 | N.E. |
| Francis Howell, Mo. | 8 | 2 | 4 | 5.0 | 1.6 | 3.1 | 1-6 | 1-8 |
| Northville, Mi. | 8 | 1 | 4 | 4.5 | 0.2 | 1.3 | K-5 | K-12 |
| Valley View, Il. | 11 | 6 | 11 | 13.0 | 8.0 | 13.0 | K-8 | K-12 |
| Prince William County, Va. | 44 | 4 | 5 | 41.0 | 3.8 | 7.2 | 1-8 | K-12 |
| Atlanta, Ga. | 185 | 25 | 13[c] | 138.0 | 13.4 | N.E.[c] | 8-12 | N.E.[c] |
| Dade County, Fl. | 225+ | 7 | 25 | 240.0 | 14.0 | 65.7 | 7-12 | K-12 |
| Hudson, N.H. | 4 | 1 | N.E. | 3.5 | 1.5 | N.E. | 9-12 | N.E. |

| Discontinued | | | | | | | | |
|---|---|---|---|---|---|---|---|---|
| Milpitas, Ca. | 16 | 16 | N.E. | 10.0 | 10.0 | N.E. | K-12 | N.E. |
| Loudoun County, Va. | 24 | 4 | N.E. | 11.6 | 3.7 | N.E. | 1-8 | N.E. |
| Virginia Beach, Va. | 48 | 4 | N.E. | 48.0 | 5.0 | N.E. | K-7 | N.E. |
| Champlain Valley, Vt. | 6 | 1 | N.E. | 3.3 | 0.034 | N.E. | 9-12 | N.E. |
| Not Implemented | | | | | | | | |
| Elk Grove, Ca. | 18 | | | 11.0 | | | | |
| Roswell, N.M. | 22 | | | 10.1 | | | | |
| Pennebury, Pa. | 18 | | | 14.0 | | | | |

[a] In thousands

[b] N.E. = no expansion

[c] Program declined in number of schools and number of students.

**Table 2-4**
**Government Support for YRS Programs**

| | State Support for YRS | | | | Federal Support for YRS | | | |
|---|---|---|---|---|---|---|---|---|
| | State Money | Technical Asst. | Legislation | Other | Title I | Title IV | Title III | Other |
| Successful | | | | | | | | |
| Hesperia, Ca. | | x | | | | | | |
| Chino, Ca. | x | x | | | | | | |
| Corona Norco, Ca. | x | | x | | | | | |
| Chula Vista, Ca. | | | x | | | | | |
| Hayward, Ca. | x | | x | | x | | x | |
| La Mesa-Spring Valley, Ca. | x | | x | | | | | |
| Pajaro Valley, Ca. | x | x | x | | | | x | |
| Colorado Springs, Co. | x | | x | | | | x | |
| Molalla, Or. | | | x | | | | | |
| Mora, Mn. | | | x | | x | | x | |
| Francis Howell, Mo. | | | | Danforth Found. Grant | | | | |
| Northville, Mi. | x | | x | | | | | |
| Valley View, Il. | | | x | | | | x | Funds for Feasibility Study |
| Prince William County, Va. | x | x | | | | | | |
| Atlanta, Ga. | | | | | x | | | |
| Dade County, Fl. | x | | x | | | | | |
| Hudson, N.H. | x | x | | | | | | |

| | | | | |
|---|---|---|---|---|
| **Discontinued** | | | | |
| Milpitas, Ca. | x | | x | |
| Loudoun County, Va. | x | | | |
| Virginia Beach, Va. | x | x | | |
| Champlain Valley, Vt. | | x | | |
| **Not Implemented** | | | | |
| Elk Grove, Ca. | | x | x | x |
| Roswell, N.M. | x | | | x |
| Pennebury, Pa. | x | | x | x |

**Table 2-5**
**Reasons for Implementing YRS**

| | Motivating Issue | | | Student Participation | |
|---|---|---|---|---|---|
| | Space/ Economic | Educational | Other | Mandatory | Voluntary |
| Successful | | | | | |
| Hesperia, Ca. | x | | | x | |
| Chino, Ca. | x | x | | | x |
| Corona Norco, Ca. | | x | | | x |
| Chula Vista, Ca. | x | | | x | |
| Hayward, Ca. | | x | | x | |
| La Mesa-Spring Valley, Ca. | x | x | | | x |
| Pajaro Valley, Ca. | x | | x[a] | | x |
| Colorado Springs, Co. | x | | | x | |
| Molalla, Or. | x | | | x | |
| Mora, Mn. | x | | | x | |
| Francis Howell, Mo. | x | | | x | |
| Northville, Mi. | x | x | | | x |
| Valley View, Il. | x | | | x | |
| Prince William County, Va. | x | x | | | x |
| Atlanta, Ga. | | x | | | x |
| Dade County, Fl. | x | | | | x |
| Hudson, N.H. | x | x | | | x |
| Discontinued | | | | | |
| Milpitas, Ca. | x | | | x | |
| Loudoun County, Va. | x | | | x | |
| Virginia Beach, Va. | x | | | x | |
| Champlain Valley, Vt. | x | x | | | x |
| Not Implemented | | | | | |
| Elk Grove, Ca. | x | x | | | |
| Roswell, N.M. | x | x | | | |
| Pennebury, Pa. | x | x | | | |

[a]Greater ethnic balance

all mandated student attendance in their programs; all those districts that implemented a YRS plan for a combination of economic and educational reasons chose to make attendance in their programs voluntary. Of the three that began YRS programs for educational reasons only, one district made its program mandatory and the other two provided for voluntary attendance. Pajaro Valley, motivated by a unique combination of factors, made its YRS program voluntary. It may be safe to assume from the relationships illustrated here that, where economy and space savings are of paramount concern, districts tend to mandate student attendance so that the maximum savings possible with a particular model are achieved. When such savings are not as immediately crucial or where educational gain is of greatest concern, districts prefer to make their YRS programs optional to students. In these cases, administrators probably feel that the advantages of YRS will become obvious and attract a satisfactory number of students to the various terms throughout the year.

School districts conduct a wide variety of activities when investigating the possibilities of YRS and planning for its actual operation (see Table 2-6). The majority of the twenty-four school districts conducted feasibility studies to weigh the pros and cons of YRS and its various models. These feasibility studies ranged in scope and content from informal and cursory looks at what was currently being done to an analysis of projected costs and impacts on school and community.

In total, of the twenty-four districts studied, sixteen conducted surveys of the community, teachers, parents, and businesses to ascertain their views on year-round schools. Previous to this, twenty-one had also either implemented or seriously investigated other ways of solving their district problems or achieving educational goals and found them unsatisfactory. Among the alternatives studied or implemented were double sessions, extended school days, or another form of year-round education.

Once a particular YRS model is selected, a school district begins to plan for its implementation. Of the twenty-one districts that implemented a YRS program, fourteen revised their school curricula in varying degrees. Eight of these districts had indicated economic and space savings to be their major goal. Their willingness to incur the initial added costs of curricular revision may indicate either that they considered such revision necessary for YRS to operate smoothly and effectively or that they may in fact have viewed YRS as an opportunity for educational innovation as well as for economizing.

Very few of the districts studied found that YRS necessitated any sort of administrative reorganization, whether this involved the hiring of new personnel or the development of a whole new office or department to handle the needs of their year-round school programs. However, almost half of the districts indicated that before the start of their YRS programs, their teachers were involved in teacher

**Table 2-6**
**School District Planning Activities**

| | Premodel Planning | | | | Implementation Planning | | | | | | | |
| | Feasibility Studies | Surveys | Alternative Solutions to Problems | Other | Curriculum | Administrative Reorganization | Teacher Training | Contract Negotiation/ Modification | Computer Scheduling | Public Relations | Surveys | Other |
|---|---|---|---|---|---|---|---|---|---|---|---|---|
| **Successful** | | | | | | | | | | | | |
| Hesperia, Ca. | x | x | x | | x | | x | | | x | | Pub. Info. Mtgs. |
| Chino, Ca. | x | x | x | | x | | x | x | | x | x | Student Orient. |
| Corona Norco, Ca. | x | | x | Pub. Mtgs. | x | x | x | | | x | | Pub. Mtgs. |
| Chula Vista, Ca. | x | x | x | | x | x | | x | | x | | |
| Hayward, Ca. | x | x | | | x | | x | | | x | | |
| La Mesa-Spring Valley, Ca. | x | x | x | Pub. Mtgs. | x | x | | x | | x | x | Parent 'Coffees' |
| Pajaro Valley, Ca. | x | x | x | | | | x | x | | x | x | Coord. of Rec. with 45-15 |
| Colorado Springs, Co. | x | | x | Pub. Mtgs. | x | | | x | | x | | Pub. Info. Mtgs. |
| Molalla, Or. | | | x | Site Visits | | | | | | | | Pub. Info. Mtgs. |
| Mora, Mn. | | | x | | | | | x | | | | Pub. Mtgs. |
| Francis Howell, Mo. | | x | x | | | | | x | | | | Pub. Mtgs. |
| Northville, Mi. | x | x | x | Pub. Relations | x | | x | x | | x | | |
| Valley View, Il. | x | x | x | Pub. Mtgs. | x | | | x | | x | | Planning YRS Rec. Activities |
| Prince William County, Va. | x | x | x | | x | | x | x | x | x | x | Parent Mtgs. |
| Atlanta, Ga. | x | | x | | x | x | | x | x | x | | Pub. & PTA Mtgs. |
| Dade County, Fl. | x | x | x | | x | | | x | | x | | |
| Hudson, N.H. | x | x | x | | x | x | | x | x | x | | Pub. Mtgs. |
| **Discontinued** | | | | | | | | | | | | |
| Milpitas, Ca. | x | x | x | Pub. & PTA Mtgs. | | | x | x | | x | x | Pub. & PTA Mtgs. |
| Loudoun County, Va. | x | | x | Site Visits | x | | x | x | | x | x | Pub. Mtgs. |
| Virginia Beach, Va. | x | x | x | | x | x | x | x | | x | x | Pub. Mtgs. |
| Champlain Valley, Vt. | | x | | | x | | | x | | x | | Pub. Mtgs. |
| **Not Implemented** | | | | | | | | | | | | |
| Elk Grove, Ca. | x | x | x | | x | | x | x | x | x | x | Financial Analysis |
| Roswell, N.M. | x | x | x | | | | | | | | | |
| Pennebury, Pa. | x | x | x | | x | | | | | x | x | Pub. Mtgs. |

training/orientation sessions to familiarize them with the operational and educational aspects of the particular plan being implemented. Some sort of teacher contract modification also occurred in the majority of school districts prior to the onset of YRS. Modifications ranged from contract renegotiation to the addition of clauses to the original contract to provide additional pay for additional days worked beyond the standard work year. Few districts found a computer necessary to handle course scheduling, entry and vacation schedules, or grade recordings.

Public relations appears to have been an important activity in all the school districts. Phone conversations with school district personnel reveal fairly general agreement that, in the end, a year-round school program must be sold to the public. Among the school districts discussed here, YRS public relations activities were conducted by school administrators and other program spokespersons who talked to community groups about the program, wrote articles for the paper, and appeared on TV or over the radio. Three districts that did not conduct a public relations effort all have successful programs, however. Two are in rural areas: Mora, Minnesota, and Molalla, Oregon. Administrators from both districts seemed to feel that the small, rural nature of their districts made it easier for residents to understand and accept year-round schools. Francis Howell is the third school district that did not conduct any sort of public relations activity. The administrator there explained that the district lacked the money to do so and that the local newspapers and the St. Louis television stations provided sufficient publicity.

Some districts conducted surveys at this point; many more informed the public of YRS by sponsoring informal parent "coffees" and public forums, opening up school board meetings for discussion of year-round schools, or giving presentations at PTA meetings. Such activities enabled those involved in the planning and implementation of a year-round school program to respond to questions from the public, provide information, and monitor the public response to the program. Two school districts indicated that at this point in their planning, they worked with local public recreation departments to plan and coordinate their activities with the new school schedule.

The amount of active, direct citizen involvement in planning for a year-round school program is quite low among the districts with successful programs (see Table 2-7). Those with citizen involvement in all phases of planning number only four. In one case, a school

**Table 2-7**
**Citizen Involvement in Planning**

| | All Phases | After Model Selection | None |
|---|---|---|---|
| Successful | | | |
| Hesperia, Ca. | | | x |
| Chino, Ca. | | | x |
| Corona Norco, Ca. | | x | |
| Chula Vista, Ca. | | | x |
| Hayward, Ca. | | | x |
| La Mesa-Spring Valley, Ca. | | | x |
| Pajaro Valley, Ca. | x | | |
| Colorado Springs, Co. | x | | |
| Molalla, Or. | | | x |
| Mora, Mn. | | | x |
| Francis Howell, Mo. | | | x |
| Northville, Mi. | x | | |
| Valley View, Il. | | | x |
| Prince William County, Va. | | | x |
| Atlanta, Ga. | | | x |
| Dade County, Fl. | | | x |
| Hudson, N.H. | x | | |
| Discontinued | | | |
| Milpitas, Ca. | | | x |
| Loudoun County, Va. | | | x |
| Virginia Beach, Va.. | | | x |
| Champlain Valley, Vt. | x | | |
| Not Implemented | | | |
| Elk Grove, Ca. | x | | |
| Roswell, N.M. | | | x |
| Pennebury, Pa. | | | x |

administrator admitted that there had been only token citizen involvement; in the three others, this involvement appears to have been an important aspect of the investigation and implementation of a particular model. In Colorado Springs, Colorado citizen involvement remains an integral part of the decision-making process regarding the day-to-day operation of the program.

Of the programs that have been discontinued, all but one, Champlain Valley, lacked any direct, active citizen involvement. As mentioned in the case study above, Champlain Valley had studied

another model of year-round schools prior to its study and implementation of Multiple Access. The community responded very
negatively to the initial study; as an administrator there pointed out,
Champlain Valley learned its lesson the hard way. In taking a second
look at year-round schools, it made certain to include the citizens in
the planning.

Citizens played key roles in the study of YRS in one of the
districts where such a program was studied but never implemented—
Elk Grove, California. In that community, as in Roswell, New
Mexico, community problems prevented implementation of a YRS
program. In both districts, the YRS programs were victims of a
credibility gap, in that the public felt suspicious of the projects and
began to mistrust what they were told regarding it. As was shown in
the case study for Elk Grove, residents believed the feasibility study
to be no more than a coverup for a decision already made—to
implement.

Active community involvement does not in itself appear to be a
guarantee of program implementation or success. Among the twenty-
four districts studied here, the lack of correlation between program
success, failure, or implementation and citizen involvement seems to
indicate the need for further study of this particular program
planning component. The dynamics of the community-school administration relationship, the way the public relations effort is handled,
and the community's perception of YRS all may be assumed to
strongly determine how a community responds to YRS and whether
or not active community involvement is necessary.

## Year-Round Schools in California

A study of YRS in California was conducted because this state has
been in the forefront of the YRS movement. The California legis-
lature has provided permissive and supportive legislation to encourage the development of year-round school programs, and the state
Department of Education actively encourages districts to study YRS.

Although Texas has passed legislation requiring shcool districts to
operate on the basis of a four-quarter system, districts are not
required to actually operate their schools during the fourth quarter.
Such legislation is not nearly as favorable to YRS programs as is that
of California. Under the Texas legislation, if a district decides to

provide a fourth quarter of study to its students, this quarter must be financed by local funds or student tuition. This stipulation appears to have effectively nullified the legislation's potential as a stimulus for YRS programs and instead seems to encourage the development of student-financed summer schools. Also, Texas does not provide the technical assistance or financial aid available to districts in California. As a result, the Texas legislation has not sparked as high a level of interest and activity in YRS as have California's laws. In fact, only one Texas district (Fort Worth) was identified as actually operating a YRS program. On the basis of these obvious differences, California was the logical choice to illustrate the impact a state government may have on YRS activity once it makes a legislative and economic commitment to YRS.

Statistical data for this section were compiled from a variety of sources. The 1973, 1974, and 1975 surveys of year-round school activities prepared by the New Jersey Department of Education yielded much information.[1] Other sources included reports by the California State Department of Education, conversations with Donald Glines of that Department, and contacts with a representative sample of California YRS programs.

More year-round school programs are operating in California than in any other state. Since the early 1970s, California has proven its primacy not only in number of YRS activities but also in the quality of legislation passed by the state government and in the constructive role its department of education has played in promoting YRS and helping districts to study and implement programs.

Year-round school programs are a recent phenomenon in California. Although a YRS program was first implemented in California in 1968, YRS did not receive much attention until the early 1970s. At this time, rapidly expanding school populations, bonded indebtedness, and inflation caused district administrators to look for practical and educationally sound solutions to these problems.

Legislation enabling school districts to implement 45-15 plans was passed in 1971, but a 1972 amendment eliminating specific mention of 45-15 allowed for broader, more flexible interpretation of year-round schools. Over the next few years additional legislation was passed as California legislators became increasingly convinced of the benefits of YRS programs. Financial aid was made available to help defray program start-up costs and to pay for the installation of air conditioning. Various provisions were mandated to ensure that citizens are made aware of any YRS program for which a district is planning. Other provisions were made to guarantee that schools with YRS get their fair share of state financial aid. Recently legislation was passed mandating districts with YRS programs to conduct evaluations of their programs at the end of the first, third, and fifth years of operation. An evaluation instrument has been developed by the state Department of Education for this purpose.

The California Department of Education encourages the development of year-round school programs as an educational option in districts where local conditions make it feasible. The Department believes that YRS has had economic and space-saving benefits and, most important, has been an effective vehicle for curriculum innovation. It feels that the complexity of today's society demands that individuals be involved in a continuous learning process that uses the total community as a learning resource and that goes beyond the "3 R's" of the traditional curriculum. In the Department's view, YRS is a means to accomplish this end.[a]

As an advocate of YRS, the Department of Education sees its responsibilities toward YRS to be the following:

to assist school districts in the exploration of YRS plans

to help interested districts plan for and implement YRS

to assist districts in evaluating their YRS programs

to help teachers understand the concept of YRS and to assist them in adjusting to a new school schedule

to work for legislation favorable to YRS

to disseminate information about YRS.

It may be said that the level of YRS activity in California over the last few years has increased dramatically, as can be seen in Figure 2-1. This sharp growth can be attributed to the active participation of the state in district YRS activities and its continued belief that YRS should be an educational option for all students.

The 1975 New Jersey survey discloses that approximately thirty-seven year-round school programs are operating in California. These

---

[a]Even so, because of lack of substantive evaluation data illustrating the benefits of YRS, Governor Brown of California nearly canceled all funding for assistance to YRS programs.

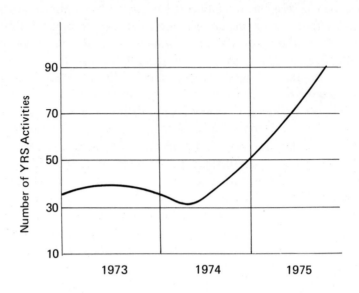

**Figure 2-1.** Interest Level in Year-Round Schools in California, 1973-1975.

programs involve about 78,460 students in grades K-12. Most programs operate at the elementary levels only and use the 45-15 plan, but two districts operate districtwide programs, and two other districts have implemented YRS on the secondary level exclusively. Of these programs, two operate flexible year-round plans, one a quinmester, and one a four-quarter plan.

The 1975 survey also shows sixty-four districts to be studying the feasibility of year-round schools. Conversations with administrators in fifteen of these districts revealed that three districts conducted feasibility studies because of school overcrowding and the desire to provide their students with a more innovative, relevant curriculum. The majority of these districts began their feasibility studies at the instigation of local school boards, who felt that they should keep abreast of interesting and promising educational innovations and who were willing to fund such studies. When beginning their feasibility studies, each of the districts surveyed all types of YRS plans and generally favored the 45-15 plan, although a few were intrigued by the possibilities of a quinmester program.

Reactions to the feasibility studies conducted by these fifteen districts varied. Three districts found their community and teachers favorable to YRS. Other districts noted that community opinions were split and teacher acceptance of YRS was hampered by their lack of knowledge about YRS and concern over how YRS would affect their salaries.

Of the districts surveyed, 85 percent indicated that during the time needed to conduct their feasibility studies the space problem in their districts appeared to ease considerably. Therefore, these districts decided not to implement YRS unless the space situation worsened. The final decisions of the other 15 percent regarding YRS hinge on the votes of their school committees.

Conversations with California educators and a review of literature developed by the state suggest future directions YRS may take in California. For instance, more districts are expressing an interest in YRS programs that are less structured and more individualized than 45-15. Such programs include the Flexible All-Year Plan, Personalized Continuous Year Plan, and the Living/Learning Plan, which uses the community as a living/learning laboratory. At the same time, districts satisfied that YRS can work in the elementary grades are beginning to examine its possibilities for their high schools.

Now that the mechanics of running a YRS program are fairly well established, the state is concentrating greater attention on the planning and construction of nontraditional school buildings that better reflect what the Department of Education hopes will become the long-term goals of YRS—to make the schools a focus of the community so as to provide continuous lifelong learning. The Bureau of School Facilities is currently providing assistance to districts that want to plan and develop creative school facilities.

The recent California legislation mandating YRS program evaluations is a step toward developing substantive data that can be used to plan and develop increasingly innovative and effective education programs. California is encouraging its districts to expand their YRS student testing beyond achievement and to begin to study the effect of YRS on other important areas of learning—the psychomotor and affective domains, human relations, and environmental awareness.

The consideration of increasingly innovative and individualized YRS plans, the planning of creative, nontraditional school buildings, the development of appropriate YRS evaluation methods—these are the directions in which California is moving. As YRS evolves, educators in the California State Department of Education hope districts will begin to resemble the schools President Lyndon B. Johnson described in a February 16, 1966, statement:

Tomorrow's school will be a school without walls . . . a school built of doors open to the entire community. . . . it will reach out to the places that enrich the human spirit—to museums, the theaters, the art galleries, the parks, the rivers, the mountains. . . . it will ally itself with the city streets, the factories, and laboratories. . . . it will be the center of community life—a shopping center of human services. . . . it will provide formal education for all. . . . it will not close its doors any more at three o'clock. It will employ its buildings round the clock, and its teachers round the year.[2]

# 3 The Recorded Impact of Year-Round Schools

To determine what impact YRS programs actually have, we reviewed the reports of evaluations conducted in the school districts under study. A number of questions were of special interest. How do parents, teachers, students, and the community feel about YRS? What effect does YRS have on student achievement? Can YRS help a community save money?

We found, as had the National Council on Year-Round Education in an assessment of selected district YRS evaluations, that most school districts evaluate the attitudes of community, teachers, and students toward YRS and that they measure the level of student achievement in YRS. Fewer districts study the financial or space savings achieved, despite the fact that these are most frequently cited as the reasons for implementing a YRS program. And some districts do not evaluate their YRS programs at all.[1]

The methodology and scope of most evaluations tend to be inadequate for truly determining the impacts of YRS. A report delivered by Elaine M. Boyce at the 1974 Western Association of Year-Round Schools Convention accurately summarized the state of assessment in year-round schools:

Over the past several years there has been a substantial increase in the amount of materials available regarding the study, planning, implementation, and evaluation of year-round school programs. Few reports, however, appear to be largely the product of objective inquiry, analysis, and evaluation. On the contrary, many of the reports appear to be subjective in viewpoint and give the indication that findings are perhaps, in some cases, offered as a means to justify actions taken toward solving some immediate and crucial problems, i.e., to provide additional needed classrooms. It is, therefore, difficult to separate fact from non-fact regarding many aspects of year-round schools.[2]

## Attitudes to YRS

School districts tend to measure the attitudes of parents, teachers, and students toward YRS some time after the first year of program

47

operation. While some districts, like Francis Howell, Missouri, continue to measure general attitudes toward YRS in each year of program operation, many districts, once satisfied that the majority of those questioned feel at least neutral about the year-round schedule as compared to the traditional school calendar, do not again study attitudes. The majority of the districts for which evaluation data were analyzed used questionnaires to measure attitudes. These questionnaires usually contain straightforward, very general questions about whether the parents like the year-round school program, whether they like the vacation schedule, whether the students miss the friends they had on the traditional school schedule, whether they like the new curricula, and so forth.

Some California districts used techniques other than simple questionnaires to assess the attitudes of parents. Hesperia, for instance, compared the level of parent involvement in school activities during the YRS school year to past school years. Chula Vista conducted telephone interviews of parents with children in YRS; and Hayward school counselors personally interviewed the parents of the sixth-graders in YRS in addition to distributing questionnaires.

Parental response in the districts studied was mixed, although positive opinions predominated. Most parents felt that their children enjoyed school more on a YRS schedule, and many indicated they enjoyed taking family vacations during times of the year when the majority of other families were not vacationing. In districts that discontinued YRS, parental apathy toward the programs (frequently coupled with teacher dissatisfaction) hastened program discontinuation.

In Francis Howell, mixed parental opinion led to a major revision in the district's YRS program. A 1974 questionnaire designed to survey parent opinions toward Francis Howell's 45-15 program showed that while most parents felt YRS was helping their children learn more than a traditional schedule did, parents of secondary school students often disagreed. Twenty-two percent of the parents of ninth-grade students in YRS felt the program actually hindered learning. The same trend was evident in opinions about the YRS vacation schedule. Parents of secondary level students tended to be more opposed to the vacation schedule of 45-15 than those with younger children. In response to the unpopularity of 45-15 at the secondary level and its perceived interference with student employment and extracurricular activities, Francis Howell removed grades

9-12 from 45-15 and allowed them to return to a traditional schedule.[3]

In contrast, parents involved in the Hayward four-quarter program overwhelmingly supported YRS—69 percent rated the program as either outstanding or excellent, and 26 percent rated it as good. They did not feel their vacation planning had been adversely affected, and 87 percent felt there had been less of a learning loss among students without the traditional summer vacation. The greatest divergence of opinion among parents concerned the issue of freedom versus discipline in Hayward's YRS program.[4]

Teacher and student attitudes toward YRS tended to be measured by how much they said they liked YRS and, in a few cases, by comparing absentee and unexcused absence records for teachers or students in YRS to the same records in a traditional program. Teachers seemed generally favorable to YRS, finding it more stimulating to them and their students. They cited the advantages of being able to use all four seasons of the year for purposes of teaching and felt that students like school on a YRS schedule better.

For instance, the Colorado Springs, Colorado district surveyed teacher attitudes toward the Concept 6 program in 1974 and 1975. The surveys found a high level of support and acceptance of YRS among involved teachers. They highly rated the attitudes of fellow teachers, parents, and students in YRS. A majority felt the quality of instruction in YRS to be excellent and that YRS facilitated curriculum development. Also, a majority of teachers felt that students forgot less over vacation periods in Concept 6 than during traditional vacation periods, that YRS had made the community more aware of educational innovations, and that YRS demanded more of their time during the evenings and on weekends. They recommended, based on their positive experiences with YRS, that the program be expanded to other schools.[5]

In Loudoun County, Virginia, where traditional teaching methods and classroom situations persisted under the new 45-15 schedule, teacher reactions to the revised schedule were in sharp contrast to the generally positive responses of the Colorado Springs teachers. Ned S. Hubbell and Associates, Inc., conducted a survey of attitudes toward YRS in Loudoun County. They found teachers in YRS to be quite divided about the program. Nearly 70 percent of the teachers said they were "generally satisfied" with working in the year-round program, but if given a choice between the district's

45-15 program and a traditional schedule, teachers were evenly divided as to which they would favor. Teachers were also nearly evenly divided in their opinions as to how effective a learning tool YRS is, how much more interesting YRS makes learning for students, whether YRS positively affects students' class behavior or attendance, whether YRS has increased their work load, and whether they are more enthusiastic about teaching in a YRS program.[6] Divergent teacher opinions and public apathy about YRS led to its demise. It may be hypothesized that apathy toward YRS was a result of the fact that while the school year was restructured, no substantive educational changes were made and that education in Loudoun County under 45-15 was not viewed positively because it was not implemented creatively.

In Prince William County, Virginia, 75 percent of the grade school students and 81 percent of the middle school students surveyed said they like YRS better than a traditional schedule or liked it about the same.[7] LaMesa-Spring Valley, California, which operates a 45-15 program similar to Prince William's, found the new vacation schedule to be the most popular aspect of YRS among its students. Students in LaMesa's program also felt they did not tire of school as quickly, that they learned more and faster, and that teachers seemed to like teaching better. When asked to suggest ways in which YRS could be improved, students requested that a greater variety of courses be offered during the intersessions between terms; that the communications system be improved so that when they were out of school they would be informed of school-related events; and that more after-school activities be provided.[8]

Four districts sent questionnaires to school principals and other administrators to learn how they felt about YRS and how it had affected their work loads, and to obtain suggestions regarding how the district's YRS program could be improved. Principals and administrators who replied generally indicated that YRS had increased their work loads, that they needed more clerical help, and that balancing students among the various YRS tracks was a major problem for them. However, they supported YRS, and in the case of Hayward, recommended YRS be expanded to additional schools, which subsequently occurred.

A few districts surveyed local business and industry to determine their opinions about YRS and its effect on their businesses. Among these, Dade County, Florida found business and industry to be neutral about YRS, aside from those that have seasonal peaks in the winter and thus favored the new schedule.[9]

In general, the attitudinal evaluations conducted by the school districts studied tended to be rather basic, unprobing surveys of individuals' opinions and provided no more than general impressions of the effect of YRS on individuals' lives. They did not provide data that explain the reasons behind specific responses nor did they ever manage to get beyond immediate emotional reactions to YRS. Questionnaires are administered systematically but unscientifically. For example, districts frequently distribute YRS parent questionnaires to their children rather than mailing out the questionnaires. Often those who are surveyed are not selected by drawing a random or stratified random sample. Survey results are often analyzed without attention being paid to response rates or to the various socioeconomic levels from which responses are elicited.

## Achievement

Achievement evaluation data for fifteen of the school districts studied were obtained. Most of these districts measured their students' achievement in YRS some time after the first year of program operation using a standardized achievement test like the California Test of Basic Skills, the Stanford Achievement Test, or the Iowa Test of Basic Skills. Generally, the test scores of YRS students were compared to the scores of similar groups of students in the district who attended non-YRS programs.

Most districts recorded mixed or inconclusive results from their testing programs. Colorado Springs noted that after two years of operation, students in YRS grades 1-3 showed higher scores overall than those in the traditional grades 1-3, but grades 4-6 showed no significant differences.[10] Northville, Michigan, on the other hand, found that after the second year of operation, YRS students scored much higher than non-YRS students on both reading and math. They found this to be true for both low, medium, and high achievers.[11] Although Loudoun County discontinued its YRS program, it nevertheless found that YRS student achievement in grades 1-6 at the end of the first and second years of program operation was slightly higher than that of comparable non-YRS students.[12]

Because of the relatively recent implementation of many programs, districts were generally reluctant to draw conclusions from test results thus far about the gains or losses of students in YRS programs. In contrast, Hayward, which began its program in 1968, has tested its students yearly and as of the May 1973, testing found certain trends to be developing. Hayward reported that the scores of YRS students in grades 1-3 were below the district and comparison group achievement levels. Teachers of children in these grades ascribe the low scores to the fact that YRS in Hayward put greater emphasis on the "affective domain" in the early grades and less emphasis on basic skills than did the traditional school program. YRS teachers stress the human relation skills of communication and sensitivity to others during these early years. Teachers and administrators in YRS have not yet found a valid method of measuring the noncognitive gains of YRS students. However, as YRS students progress through grades 4 to 8, they show major gains in reading, mathematics, and language skills. Overall they tend to achieve higher scores on tests than do comparable groups of non-YRS students. On the basis of the achievement evidence, Hayward concluded that the longer a child attends the YRS program, the higher the child's achievement scores will be.[13]

In their most recent evaluation study, Hayward administrators commented on the difficulty of measuring the noncognitive effects of their YRS program and pointed out that they could not obtain a valid measurement of the quantitative educational effects of the additional twenty days' instruction time per year provided by YRS. They also stated that they had not yet determined a valid way of measuring the effect of YRS on summer learning loss.

These comments by Hayward point out the inadequacies of trying to validly measure the achievement of students in YRS programs that have sought to restructure their curricula and provide innovative learning experiences. Standardized achievement tests were not developed to measure achievement in affective and noncognitive areas.

More generally, when school districts test achievement, the same test is not always used in both the pre-YRS and post-YRS testing periods, nor are the same tests administered to all grade levels in YRS: comparisons of test results are therefore limited. Therefore, the fact that student achievement in YRS has thus far not provided overall dramatic gains cannot be interpreted as an indictment of YRS. Carefully administered evaluation tools that adequately measure the hypothesized educational benefits of YRS and that measure the overall difference YRS makes in students' lives must be developed before realistic conclusions may be drawn about YRS.

## Financial Impacts

Financial evaluations were available for eleven of the districts studied. Five indicated that they had not conducted financial evaluations of their YRS programs, despite the fact that economic savings had been at least a partial reason for their implementation of YRS.

Most districts conduct their own financial evaluations. Those districts for which financial data are available generally studied the per-pupil or operational cost of YRS as compared either to costs incurred by the school prior to YRS or to those incurred by a comparable school in the district operating on a traditional schedule.

District results varied but most found that while operational costs tended to increase with YRS, the overall savings that resulted from not having to build a new school or to add room onto a school made YRS a money saver in the long run. For instance, Hesperia found that after the first year of operation its costs increased by $16,949. This increase was ascribed to paying teachers for twelve months of work and providing them with increased benefits, as well as to increased bus utilization. However, when Hesperia compared the operational cost increase to the projected $192,000 it would have cost to provide additional space, YRS was seen as providing a considerable savings.[14] Chula Vista found that its per-pupil costs were the same in both YRS and traditional programs, but estimated that YRS was saving $2 million in capital building costs in the long run.[15]

Education Turnkey Systems, Inc., conducted Prince William County's financial evaluation. They estimated the long-run equilibrium costs of school operation with 45-15 as opposed to a traditional schedule, considering the costs of staff, supplies, and plant maintenance by developing two cost models for comparison. They found that overall 45-15 lowered per-pupil costs by providing 4.9 percent more intensive use of labor and 4.7 percent more intensive use of school facilities than would be possible by operating on a traditional schedule.[16]

Prince William County also conducted a separate energy consumption study comparing amount of energy consumed in a traditional school year to that consumed on 45-15. The total kilowatthours consumed per student day for schools on 45-15 and on a traditional schedule were calculated. It was found that the total amount of energy consumed in a year was greater for the YRS schools, but on a per student-day basis energy consumption was the same.[17] Finally, Virginia Beach, Virginia determined that by operating on a YRS schedule it was saving, in terms of capital and operating costs, eight dollars per student as compared to operating on a traditional schedule.[18]

It must be said that, in general, cost data from financial evaluations are unsatisfactory sources of information about YRS. The accounting systems used by districts to record YRS costs vary greatly, and a consistent cost allocation or attribution method could not be discerned from reported district evaluation data. Lack of comparability prevents a determination of whether YRS is a cost-effective method of operating, and if so, under what conditions.

## Conclusions

As a whole, YRS evaluations do not reveal as much as could be wished about the importance of YRS and are therefore not useful planning tools. They generally evaluate only the most obvious elements of a YRS program and have not conclusively answered the three basic questions districts pose when initially studying YRS: Will it be favorably received? Will it affect students' learning? Will it save money?

Quite apart from the limited value of the findings in the evaluations studied here, school districts have not yet attempted to investigate a wide range of possible YRS impacts, a number of which are discussed in Chapter 4. These unexplored areas are important not only to the school district and community but also to the federal government, since district YRS activities may be affecting the outcomes or intersecting the activities of various federal programs. It is these areas of unexplored impact that may reveal most about the educational and social benefits of YRS. For instance, relatively few secondary level YRS programs exist, and those that do exist have hardly been studied. Little if any attention has been paid to the effect of YRS on drop-out rates and student motivation or the success a school district like Atlanta has had in facilitating work/study at the high school level. The YRS program in Atlanta may in effect be accomplishing the goals of the federal government's career education program; or it may be an ideal situation in which a federally funded career education program could be implemented.

"Science," as scientists are wont to say, "grows by accretion." The immense amount of information so willingly provided by the school districts has at least helped formulate new questions and ideas about the potential of this important grass-roots educational movement. It is to these new questions and potential impacts that we now turn.

# 4

## YRS Issues Refined

Thus far, we have kept close to the data. This chapter makes some extrapolations that are subject to interpretation. We feel they are warranted; they should at least stimulate further inquiry. In any case, a wide-ranging presentation of the questions and issues involved in YRS can hardly avoid such areas of dispute.

Since the real and potential impact of YRS is so complex, this discussion is not exhaustive. Moreover, the particular concerns of a school district will vary depending on which YRS model is under consideration. The experiences of YRS schools and the literature on the subject have suggested a five-fold division: cost issues, educational issues, YRS and parents, YRS and teachers, and YRS and the community.

### Cost Issues

This section discusses the principles and issues involved in analyzing the costs of conversion to YRS. It is not intended as a step-by-step guide to cost analysis.[1] However, since an analysis of projected costs will be a major part of any YRS feasibility study and of most evaluations of YRS programs, it is important that those not familiar with economic analyses understand how the costs of various calendars are compared.

#### Defining the Costs of Education

When school cost analysts attempt to determine the costs of education, they use such measures as the annual budget for the schools or annual spending per pupil. Whether a measure is appropriate depends on the questions one wishes to ask about school costs; generally, however, the most useful measure is the cost of providing one year of education (175-180 classroom days) to one student during a calendar year. Although the student only attends class for nine months, it still costs money to maintain the school facilities during the remaining three months of vacation. Calculation of the annual cost per student is no different for YRS than for traditional school calendar (TSC) schools. In both systems a student receives 175-180 days of instruction a year while the school is maintained for all twelve months.

An overly simplistic and erroneous cost analysis occasionally encountered in discussions about YRS uses the total cost of operating a school for a year. For instance, a YRS feasibility study may calculate the cost of operating the school on TSC and on YRS and find that the total YRS cost is higher. While true as far as it goes, this analysis leaves out the critical fact that the YRS plan changes the number of students that can be educated in the school in twelve months. To take a purely hypothetical example, if YRS increases the total cost of running the school by 10 percent, but provides for the education of 30 percent, more students than TSC, YRS is cheaper because the cost of education per pupil is lower.

Cost analysis gets especially tricky when YRS is proposed as a way to relieve overcrowded TSC schools. Again, suppose that a school has been operating on split-shifts (half-day sessions) because there are too many students and not enough classrooms. If a YRS plan enables the existing buildings to accommodate all the students in full-time classes, what effect will this have on school costs? In this case, both the total school budget and the per-pupil cost will increase when YRS is compared to the split-session TSC school. But once the community decides that split sessions are unacceptable, the comparison must be made between the costs of alternative methods for relieving the overcrowding, not between the costs of operating split sessions and of providing full-day classes. Hence the projected cost of YRS must be compared to the projected cost of building new TSC schools. Both will cost more than half-day sessions, but YRS will invariably be cheaper.

These two brief examples have shown how cost per pupil can go down or up while the total school budget goes up. It is also possible, when enrollment is declining, for per-pupil costs to increase when the total budget declines (see below). The point is that total school costs and costs per pupil may change in different ways; school administrators or citizens who are interested in what the taxpayers are getting for their money should generally use annual per-pupil costs as the basis for comparison.

Another way of thinking about costs is to divide the various types of expenses schools have into fixed or variable costs. Simply put, a fixed cost is something that must be paid whether the school is used or not, while a variable cost is something that has to be paid only when the school is in use. For example, the debt incurred in constructing a school building has to be paid off whether the building is used for classes or sits idle during a summer vacation. Teachers' salaries are a variable cost; they only have to be paid when the teachers are actually working.

The facilities of TSC schools are idle for long stretches of the year; YRS facilities are not. Thus the cost savings of YRS come about by reducing fixed costs. Since more pupils are educated using the same facilities as before, fixed costs per pupil drop. Similarly, the proportion of fixed costs in the annual school budget decreases. The great bulk of a district's fixed costs is represented by capital costs—the physical facilities and equipment, such as buildings and buses needed by the district. By making it unnecessary to construct expensive new school buildings, YRS effects its most dramatic savings in capital costs, both per pupil and as a proportion of the annual budget.

When the effects of YRS on variable costs are discussed, it will be convenient to distinguish two kinds of variable costs—operating costs and start-up costs. Operating costs are pretty much the same as variable costs and refer to what it costs to run the school. Start-up costs occur only once, when a new program is undertaken. Start-up costs can be thought of as the cost over and above normal operating costs that occur when the educational program is changed from one form to another.

*Capital Costs*

The savings in capital costs resulting from conversion to YRS have already been stressed. Nevertheless, these will be somewhat reduced in many cases by the necessity to air-condition YRS buildings. The cost of air conditioning is, however, quite small when compared to the cost of building a new school. There are several other factors that should be considered in determining how much the cost of air conditioning offsets the savings in construction costs. Depending on climate and fuel costs, it may be cheaper to air-condition existing buildings during the summer than to heat a new building during the winter. In many areas of the country, it would be unfair to attribute all the cost of air-conditioning the schools to the YRS program. In these schools, effective learning often comes to a halt in late spring and does not resume until late fall as a result of high temperatures. During these periods, especially in elementary schools, children are only warehoused in hot classrooms.

Some of the cost of air conditioning must therefore be assigned to the part of the school year that would also fall in the TSC, because part of the benefit occurs there. More and more TSC schools are being built with air conditioning anyway. If a district considering YRS or new construction would probably air-condition the new building, the cost of air-conditioning existing buildings for YRS use should not be charged to YRS.

Parenthetically, Molalla Elementary School near Portland, Oregon avoided the need for air conditioning during the summer by changing the hours of school to 7:00 am to 1:30 pm. Thus children left school before the heat of the day would have made air conditioning necessary. While this approach would not work in all areas of the country, it is a good illustration of what can be accomplished when people break the force of TSC habit.

A final note regarding capital costs: if YRS is used as a temporary rather than as a permanent solution to overcrowding, the money saved by operating a YRS program for a few years until the district can better afford to build new buildings and change back to TSC may well be lost to inflated construction costs.

*Operating Costs*

The experiences of a number of schools suggest that changing to YRS can produce savings in operating costs as well as in capital costs. While operating cost savings of as much as 10 percent have been reported, savings in the neighborhood of 4 to 5 percent are more usual. Nevertheless, most schools report increased operating costs with YRS.

What happens to operating costs is complex and depends on a number of factors. First, it seems clear that certain categories of operating costs will decline under YRS. Per-pupil expenses attributable to the depreciation of idle facilities and the cost of maintaining idle facilities over the TSC summer vacation will be saved. If the energy consumption cost of air conditioning is less than the cost of heating (or if no air conditioning is needed), per-pupil energy cost will decline. If teachers are offered the option of teaching more than the traditional nine months, certain types of personnel costs will be saved (social security/retirement contributions, payroll preparation, health insurance), since fewer teachers will be needed than would be required for the same student body in TSC.

Furthermore, the general experience of YRS schools has been that it is unnecessary to hire more administrators than were used in TSC. School administrative staff, who generally work year round in TSC to begin with, seem to be able to combine their previous summer duties with running an operating school under YRS. Consequently, the school can educate more students for the same administrative cost, thereby reducing the per-pupil cost of administration.

Savings are not guaranteed in any of these operating cost categories except for depreciation. Much depends on the circumstances (climate and air conditioning) and on how well the YRS program was planned.

On the debit side, increased operating costs can be expected in a number of areas. If all the schools in a district do not convert to YRS, it is desirable to offer parents the choice of sending their children to either a YRS or a TSC school (see the section on YRS and parents). Thus, additional transportation costs will occur when students who live in the YRS zone are bused to a TSC school. If the YRS plan allows parents complete freedom in deciding when their children attend school, force of habit will preserve TSC attendance in the year-round school. It will then be very expensive to operate the school over the summer when only a few students are attending.

Some increase in clerical staff may be necessary to handle the additional paper work that will probably result from the more frequent starts and stops in the school year brought about by YRS. Also, converting to YRS is generally accompanied by extensive curriculum reform. These curricular revisions probably are a major factor in schools where operating costs increase. (It is arguable whether these costs should be assigned to YRS—see below.)

In conclusion, whether operating costs increase or decrease will largely be determined by how well the school plans its YRS program. To good planners, YRS can offer opportunities to save on operating costs that would not be available in TSC schools.

*Problems in Assigning Costs*

One problem in assigning costs has to do with start-up costs for a YRS program, the one-time expenses necessary to change the school from TSC to YRS. Start-up costs include such things as rescheduling, negotiating new teacher contracts, holding public meetings, informing the public, conducting a feasibility study, restructuring the curriculum, planning new bus routes, etc. Since these are one-time costs, they will affect the total budget only once, at the beginning of (or the year before) the YRS program.

The effect start-up costs have on per-pupil costs depends on how many years the YRS program operates. Since they affect the entire life of the program, they should be spread over the entire lifetime of the YRS program. Therefore, what start-up costs add to per-pupil costs decreases the longer the YRS operates. Feasibility studies conducted to estimate the costs of YRS should place start-up costs in a separate category and then amortize them over the estimated number of years the YRS program will operate.

Many different items in the school budget will be affected by the change-over to YRS. And even after YRS cost analysts have made out a list of budget areas that are affected by a calendar change, they must still determine whether each area is an inevitable consequence of YRS or a change that, while desirable for other reasons, is made at the same time as the calendar change because it is easy to do so. Curriculum revision is especially difficult to sort out. Clearly, the curriculum must be handled differently under YRS than under TSC, but how much change is the minimum needed to adjust to the new calendar?

In many cases the TSC text can be divided into four, five, or six parts so that each part can be covered during one YRS attendance period. But once the reform process is started, abandoning the TSC text for modular or individualized curricula becomes increasingly attractive for other pedagogical reasons. The change to YRS may facilitate accomplishing these other objectives, but if the YRS does not absolutely require these changes, it is not fair to lay all the cost of the change to the YRS program.

The matter is difficult, since sweeping curriculum change that would ordinarily be difficult to bring about can often be more easily made under the guise of YRS, especially when "blame" for the cost of the curriculum reform can be placed on YRS. But, in all justice, advocates of YRS who have continually emphasized its value as a way of introducing curricular reform should not wash their hands when the bills arrive.

## Cost Controversies

Many schools faced by rising enrollments or overcrowding have saved considerable sums by switching to YRS rather than building new TSC buildings. Some might argue that YRS is no longer a viable option, since overcrowding was a temporary phenomenon due to the post-World War II baby boom. Now that the baby-boom students are well through school, enrollments are declining, and the trend in births suggests that declining enrollment will continue for at least the next decade.

Of course, this demographic argument ignores the role of migration. Though out-migration may accelerate the decline in enrollment in some schools, other schools may be swamped with the children of families settling in the area.

More importantly, though, this argument overlooks a crucial aspect of YRS: the efficient use of school facilities. In fact, by using their facilities efficiently, school districts can deal better with declining enrollments as well.

Suppose a community has three elementary schools, each filled to capacity with 300 students, for a total elementary enrollment of 900. Assume that enrollment begins to decline. When the decline in enrollment reaches about 11 percent, or a total enrollment of 800 students, YRS offers an alternative to continued TSC use of partially empty schools. If one school is closed and the two remaining schools are converted to a 45-15 plan, the 800 students can be accommodated in two fully used schools rather than in three partially empty TSC schools.

Just as it is inefficient to let schools sit idle for the three summer months, so it becomes increasingly inefficient to educate each student when the school facility is not used to capacity. When enrollments decline, changing some schools to YRS permits the closing of superfluous schools sooner than would otherwise be possible. And closing schools when enrollment is declining saves money in two ways.

If the capital costs of the facility are divided evenly among all the students using the facility (per-pupil capital costs), the cost of educating each student increases as enrollment falls, since capital costs don't change, and they must be divided among fewer students than before. Second, operating costs per pupil will also increase as the school is used at less than capacity. Empty classrooms require a minimum level of maintenance—heat, sweeping the floors, replacing broken windows, etc.—and the cost of maintaining empty classrooms must be borne by the students remaining in the building. (Thus, per-pupil costs can rise even if the total budget is declining.)

The final step in realizing cost savings from closing schools when enrollment is declining is to sell or rent the school to a business or other institution. Although it may be cheaper to maintain a completely closed school than one in partial use, an empty school still costs money. Construction bonds must be paid off whether the school is in use or not, and even totally empty buildings require some maintenance. If the building is paid for, it is still a waste to let it sit empty: the money tied up in the building could be put to other uses. By shortening the length of time needed to turn underutilized schools into income producers for the school system by sale or rental, conversion to YRS offers very definite economic advantages to schools facing enrollment declines.

It may at first seem surprising that controversy exists over the cost savings aspect of using school facilities and equipment over the summer. After all, few industries would consider letting their factories sit idle for one-fourth of the year. Advocates of YRS claim that savings would result from the more efficient summer use of idle buildings, textbooks, school buses, instructional materials, and equipment. The counterclaim is that full-time use of facilities and equipment will wear them out faster: therefore, no money is saved because replacements have to be bought sooner in YRS than in TSC.

This argument ignores several points. First, textbooks and many instructional materials are usually replaced because they are outdated, not because they are worn out. Many schools replace out-of-date textbooks almost in secret to avoid being accused of throwing away perfectly good books. So YRS can indeed save money by more fully using these materials.

Second, it costs money just to have things standing idly by. Even though schools are unoccupied by students in summer, they require a minimal level of maintenance work to keep them up. Also, the effects of weather on the buildings and buses continue year-round, whether they are used or not. Physical facilities and buses will also lose value during idle periods through depreciation. Although less obvious than other expenses, depreciation is nevertheless one of the costs of operating a school that continues even if the school is not in use.

Opponents of YRS argue that it is not true that TSC schools sit empty during the summer. They are used for summer school, special events, and the like. Therefore, conversion to YRS would mean the elimination of these worthwhile programs. The amounts of money supposedly saved by conversion to YRS must also be reduced to reflect the extent to which TSC buildings are used over the summer.

However, conversion to YRS does not necessarily mean these special programs have to be discontinued. When schools are converted to YRS, there is usually some excess space that can be set aside for special programs. For instance, many 45-15 schools operate remedial extra sessions all year long. Called "intersessions," the remedial classes are conducted during each group's vacation period.

Conversion to YRS does change one aspect of how TSC schools are used during the summer. The school administration no longer has to think up special summer uses of the school to avoid taxpayer reaction to empty schools. Extra programs can be judged on their merit and not by whether they make a good public impression.

*Conclusions about Costs*

In conclusion, what can be said about the effect of YRS on school costs? The experience of existing YRS programs shows that YRS saves on construction costs. The effect of YRS on operating costs is more complex. Although most schools experience an overall increase in operating costs when changing to YRS, the experience of schools that have managed to reduce operating costs suggests that a 5 percent reduction in operating costs is a reasonable expectation. Certain cost categories will yield savings in YRS while other costs will increase. On balance, it seems as if a slight reduction in operating costs per pupil can be achieved for those budget items that are invariably and necessarily affected by YRS. However, the final impact on operating costs is determined by other changes made for convenience' sake during implementation of YRS, or by improper planning.

**Educational Issues**

Although schools generally adopt a YRS schedule to solve over-crowding or economic problems, YRS is sometimes adopted as a technique of educational reform to bring about any one of a number of its hypothesized educational benefits. Even YRS programs begun solely for economic reasons experience its other effects. A case in point is the relationship between YRS and individualized instruction and ungraded classes.

Many educators argue that schools could be greatly improved if students were not age-grouped and force-fed a common curriculum. Rather, students would learn better if each child were able to proceed through the curriculum at his or her own pace. Although there seems to be a general acceptance of this philosophy among educational authorities, individualized instruction programs have proved to be very difficult to implement in practice.

Part of the reason may be that the practice of batch processing students is an integral part of the whole structure and operation of the traditional school. For example, the normal textbook or reading series is designed so that the average student can complete it in the traditional nine months of school. Nor will simply replacing the textbooks necessarily result in an individualized program. Instead, the teacher, accustomed to traditional ways, may simply say to the class, "All right, children, open your individualized workbooks to page 31 and begin."

Conversion to YRS can help to implement an individualized instructional program by breaking up the business-as-usual atmosphere of the TSC school. Because traditional, nonindividualized curricula are geared to a traditional nine-month school calendar, they do not always fit into a YRS calendar; but even if they do, individualized instruction clearly fits better. The task of breaking a traditional nine-month instructional program into nine-week segments is often not easy, while an individualized program can be stopped and started almost at will.

The ease with which an individualized curriculum fits into a YRS calendar and the comparative difficulty of transferring a nine-month instructional program to a YRS setting leads to consequences that may not have been anticipated if the YRS program was begun solely for cost reasons. The logic of the YRS schedule, once established, compels major curriculum reform. The paradox of YRS is that a conservative community that would never have accepted radical curriculum changes in TSC schools (and that perhaps regularly defeated bond issues) will easily accept these changes in a YRS program initiated to cope with overcrowding. This section deals with a number of other such effects of YRS.

## Summer Learning Loss

An interesting educational issue involving YRS concerns the summer learning loss phenomenon. The first weeks (even months) of TSC school in the fall are spent in resocializing the students to school life and in reviewing material that has been forgotten over the summer. This time is wasted in that no new learning goes on. Advocates of YRS argue that after shorter vacations, returning students will still remember what they learned during the prior school session. It must be emphasized that this is an untested hypothesis—no definitive study of the effect of YRS on summer learning loss has been made. The few extant studies of achievement test scores in YRS have not been set up to test for summer learning loss effects; test results vary, but most are inconclusive.

The summer learning loss hypothesis becomes particularly interesting when applied to disadvantaged students. It has been argued that the home environment plays a critical role in determining the child's academic performance. Middle-class children do better in school than do the children of the poor because middle-class parents are more likely to read books, for instance, and to encourage their children to read books. The middle-class home environment, it is argued, provides more support for the effects of school over the summer than does the disadvantaged home. Therefore, summer learning loss should be worse in students from a disadvantaged background than for middle-class students.

There is some evidence that this is so. Thomas and Pelavin[2] found that Title I programs, the federal government's major compensatory education program, are quite successful during the school year. It is not unreasonable for a Title I program to produce 1.3 to 1.5 months of academic gain for each month of instruction during the school year. However, the portion of this gain that is in excess of the normal gain for disadvantaged students not in compensatory programs (about .7 months per month) vanishes over the summer.

Consequently, disadvantaged children can spend several years in a compensatory program, showing spectacular gains each year, but finishing no better off than if they had never been in the program in the first place. If YRS does indeed eliminate summer learning loss, the result in compensatory education programs would be to carry the program's gains over from year to year.

However, Hamson[3] holds that YRS aggravates the problem of summer learning loss. Psychological research shows that forgetting occurs most rapidly during the early stages after learning and then more and more slowly as time goes on. This extinction curve is shown graphically in Figure 4-1. The amount forgotten over the TSC summer is the distance between points $A$ and $C$ on the vertical scale. The amount forgotten during a three-week break under a 45-15 YRS plan is the vertical distance between points $A$ and $B$. While $AB$ is clearly less than $AC$, YRS forgetting ($AB$) happens four times a year. Therefore, the total amount forgotten in YRS is four times $AB$, considerably more than $AC$.

While this hypothesis raises serious questions about the effects of YRS, it should be placed in perspective. There are three reasons why the extinction phenomenon must be considered speculation rather than fact. First, the extinction curve characterizes the behavior of rats learning mazes and of college students memorizing lists of nonsense syllables, over short periods of time, under very carefully controlled laboratory situations. The same phenomenon may not happen to children in schools, though it's worth thinking about. Second, one can hypothesize just the opposite using different theories; what is needed is data. And third, as mentioned, most test results are inconclusive on this point.

Though the analysis Hamson presents to support his hypothesis is inappropriate, his contention that YRS makes summer learning loss worse merits study. So does the argument that YRS reduces summer learning loss. The available evidence indicates that there is no need for parents or schools to panic—YRS does not seem to be harmful.

*Measuring Student Achievement*

The summer learning loss phenomenon aside, there seems to be no reason to expect YRS academic achievement to be any different from TSC (unless YRS is an integral part of total curriculum reform,

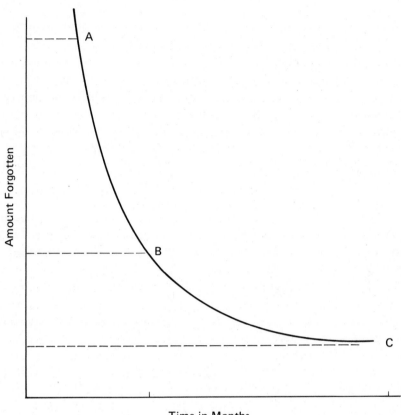

Source: Derived from: R.L. Hamson, "Year-Round School: Political Football or Taxpayer's Dream?" Paper presented at the Annual Meeting of the Operations Research Society of America, Western Section, 1976.

**Figure 4-1.** Forgetting over Time (Extinction Curve).

which can be expected to improve student achievement). Consequently, the question to be asked in evaluating YRS is not whether it leads to higher test scores but rather whether it has harmful effects (lowered test scores) on students. As long as student achievement is the same for both TSC and YRS, the choice between the two can be safely made on other grounds such as cost or more flexible use of time. The existing evidence supports the conclusion that YRS is not harmful, but it must again be noted that no studies have addressed the summer learning loss hypothesis. Therefore, it seems reasonable to conclude that YRS is academically safe; whether it is superior to TSC is still an open question.

When is the appropriate time to evaluate the YRS program? The first year or two of a poorly thought-out YRS program may be so hectic and disorganized that learning suffers. On the other hand, a well-planned and smoothly implemented program may produce falsely high gains in achievement. One of the few firm conclusions that can be drawn from the long history of research on educational innovation is that if you do something different, test scores will go up a little. The first year in a well-run YRS program is likely to be a novel experience, and any improvement in achievement scores could be due to the novelty effect rather than to any inherent superiority of the YRS program.

Another problem in picking the right time to evaluate the academic impact of YRS is that many of the changes (for instance, in curriculum) triggered by the calendar change can take years to work themselves out. As long as this process is incomplete, evaluation would be premature. On the other hand, a school is a dynamic place; one could wait forever before the YRS program finally settled down.

An evaluation should certainly be done at the end of the first year to be sure the program isn't so messed up that it is harmful, but the first-year evaluation should also be followed by at least a third-year evaluation. Three years seems a reasonable length of time for any novelty effects to have worn off and for the YRS program to have settled down into a state of regular operation. Fortunately for those interested in evaluating the effects of YRS on learning, the state of California requires schools that have received state aid in changing to YRS to conduct evaluations in the first, third, and fifth years of operation. As the pool of data grows in California as more and more schools pass these milestones, we may begin to learn something about how YRS affects achievement.

*Practical Effects of YRS Schedules*

Under most YRS schedules, a student could complete primary and secondary school in fewer years than possible in TSC. By skipping vacation sessions, a student on the 45-15 plan could move from the first grade through high school in about nine years rather than twelve. (Note that such a schedule would still include about 2.5 to 3 weeks vacation per year.) Though accelerated completion of school lets students progress at their own pace and reduces boredom, very young high school graduates will probably be immature. Furthermore, current employment requirements, state child labor laws, and college admission standards pose difficulties for the exceptionally young high school graduate.

Nevertheless, as an option available under YRS, early graduation must count as a benefit, since it increases the flexibility of schooling and broadens the student's range of choices. School counselors must make it clear to students considering an accelerated program and to their parents what the problems will be so that a realistic choice can be made.

A more common problem faced by parents is at what age to put their children in school. Parents of a five-year-old may feel their child is too immature for school, and yet be concerned that he or she will be too mature by the following September. YRS schedules eliminate this problem, which is unavoidable in TSC. By providing several opportunities during the year to begin school, YRS almost guarantees that children can begin school when they are ready for it.

This flexibility of the YRS calendar can be a problem when a student from a TSC school transfers to a YRS program at mid-year. However, transferring from one TSC school to another is not without problems, since it is unlikely the two curricula will match. In either case the source of the problem is likely to be the curriculum, not the schedule. Similarly, the four to six YRS graduations throughout the year may leave the college-bound graduate with a longer wait before starting college than in TSC. (Even this is not inevitable, since most colleges provide entry points at various times during the year.) However, the college-bound graduate's loss is the job-seeker's gain. It will be easier for industry to absorb fewer applicants at spaced intervals than to cope with a once-a-year glut of new graduates.

Another problem with YRS schedules may arise when communities planning a YRS program try to reconcile the differing educational needs of high schools and elementary schools. The 45-15 plan has been particularly popular in elementary schools, but YRS high schools have generally found it unsatisfactory because of its short school attendance sessions. Many high school subjects are thought to be difficult to break up into 45-day segments and sequencing courses becomes harder. Consequently, high schools prefer the YRS schedules like the Quinmester plan.

Totally YRS districts are still very rare, and there is little experience to go by in deciding how to best schedule both elementary and high schools on the same YRS plan. However, the experience of high schools on some of the more flexible YRS calendars indicates that following the "proper" sequence both within and among courses is more of a habit than on inherent requirement of the subject matter. It will take more time, effort, and money to modularize or individualize the high school curriculum than to continue teaching in the same old way, but it can be and has been done with great success.

*Possible Detrimental Effects*

Some YRS schools report more disciplinary problems; others report fewer. YRS should tend to reduce disciplinary problems associated with end of the year boredom and with resocialization to school after a long three-month vacation. On the other hand, disciplinary problems could increase during the summer sessions until going to school in the summer becomes habit.

Among the reported problems associated with YRS schools are the following: more impersonal relations between teachers and students, when changing teachers occurs more frequently than in TSC; students who are on vacation sometimes hang around the school and disrupt classes; disruption of extracurricular activities as a result of the frequent changes in the student body; and insufficient demand for some courses, which makes it impossible to schedule them every session, resulting in some scheduling problems for students. All that can be said is that those planning to implement YRS should plan to deal with these possible problems.

## YRS and Parents

A number of schools have surveyed parental attitudes toward YRS as part of a YRS feasibility study or a YRS evaluation (see Chapter 3). These surveys suggest an interesting phenomenon—a majority of parents not in YRS oppose the idea, whereas most YRS parents prefer YRS to TSC. It must be repeated that these surveys are often of very questionable scientific validity, but since the finding turns up in several different places, it is at least worth some consideration.

This phenomenon is probably the result of force of habit. People are comfortable with their habits, and they are understandably suspicious of things that promise to upset their customary way of life. The traditional school calendar is a habit, and advocates of YRS need to recognize this point. The important thing to note is that most parents prefer YRS when they have had the opportunity to directly experience both schedules.

Although there is almost no research on the subject, we think parents who have tried both TSC and YRS generally prefer YRS because:

1. Learning to live with YRS isn't really all that difficult. It is usually just a case of learning how to reschedule certain family activities.

2. Shorter vacations, even though more frequent, turn out to be less tiring to both parents and children than does a three-month summer break.

3. The parents can see some positive educational effects in their children. Parents notice that their children don't get as bored with school and that they settle into school faster after vacation. Also, parents don't see any harmful effects on their children.

4. Parents discover that they like the pattern of leisure time in YRS. Families can do a lot more with four three-week vacations spread across the year than they can with one three-month summer. Avoiding long lines at Disneyland is no minor contribution to having a happy vacation.

Almost all effects of YRS on the parents depend on the exact YRS plan used, the distribution of the children's ages, and the nature of the parents' work. For instance, certain YRS arrangements can disrupt family activities and cause considerable problems in planning family vacations (e.g., children in the same family attend different schools, which have different calendars). This problem is most likely to occur when there are children of both high school and elementary school age. When children in the same family have different vacation schedules, such problems as planning a family vacation or finding baby sitters become all the more complicated.

In view of these and other potential problems, school districts should offer parents the choice of enrolling their children in TSC or year-round schools, especially since overcrowding can almost always be relieved by converting only some of the school buildings to YRS (indeed, converting all the schools to YRS could lead to problems of over-capacity and unused space). Aside from increasing options in education, offering parents a choice in which calendar their child attends makes it easier to get parental acceptance of the change to YRS. Some parents have insurmountable problems in adjusting to the YRS schedule. Their acceptance of the program will be facilitated if they are offered an opportunity to continue their children's education in TSC. On the other hand, some parents who live in TSC attendance zones may prefer YRS for their child. Their support of the change in other attendance zones will increase if they can send their children to the YRS school. Some YRS schools have accommodated parents who are adamant for TSC by including TSC classrooms within the YRS school. It should be pointed out that this solution requires an individualized program, since the number of TSC students attending the YRS school is too small to support separate age-graded classrooms.

When YRS is used to relieve overcrowding, parents cannot be given complete freedom of choice between TSC or YRS programs: the strength of the TSC habit is too strong. Fortunately, most parents are willing to try YRS when it is mandated by the school. It also appears that parents are more strongly opposed to busing their children away from their neighborhood school than they are opposed to YRS. Therefore, when the choice is between a neighborhood YRS school or a distant TSC school, only a small proportion of parents opt for TSC.


## YRS and Teachers

While the pattern of attitudes of teachers toward YRS parallels that of parents—those who have actually experienced YRS are more favorable toward YRS than those who have only had experience with TSC—teachers seem to be generally more hostile to YRS than parents. The negative reaction of teachers toward YRS is not well understood and is somewhat puzzling since YRS can offer teachers a number of advantages over TSC. To mention one, many teachers find that their income from teaching in a TSC is too low and therefore take a second job during the summer. Their summer jobs are usually unrelated to the teacher's training and teaching skills. But in a properly designed YRS, teachers can work full-time (twelve months a year, with about 3.5 weeks of vacation) at teaching, not painting houses over the summer.

Again, teachers who elect to teach only nine months can arrange their schedules so that those three months come at any time of the year. If a teacher would rather have more frequent but shorter vacations, she or he can have a teaching schedule that corresponds to the schedule of one of the student groups, teaching for forty-five days and then having a three-week vacation.

The second alternative is appealing in view of the lack of discipline in students. The daily battle against the barbarians gets the teacher down, and breaking the school year up into forty-five-day segments with three-week vacations in between may be very restorative.

Curriculum revision is another area where YRS offers promise to teachers. YRS leads to major changes in curriculum as part of the process of adapting to the new schedule. These changes are so sweeping and must be done in such a short time that the school administration can't do it alone; hence teachers have to be included in the process. Although it may seem obvious that those who must teach the curriculum should have a voice in planning the curriculum, this is often not the case in TSC. Nor is this a planned-for consequence of YRS: like curriculum reform in a program undertaken for economy's sake, it just sort of happens.

YRS may make it more difficult for teachers to complete required postgraduate work (traditionally done during the summer). However, careful planning can mitigate the extent of this problem.

Again, YRS may force teachers to change classrooms several times during the year. But schools can take steps to minimize the problems of moving. For example, a very effective step in many YRS schools has been to mount the teacher's classroom furniture (desk, filing cabinets, bookshelves) on rollers. At the end of a session, the teacher just puts things away and the custodial staff rolls everything to the teacher's new classroom or to storage if the teacher is going on vacation that session.

A probable (and unwelcome) consequence of YRS is that teachers will have to spend more time on bookkeeping. However, any increased work load resulting from implementation will probably be brought up during contract renegotiations.

## YRS and the Community

Because a great many social institutions are organized to mesh their activities with the TSC schedule, the spread of YRS would have effects throughout the community. For instance, the traditional industrial vacation pattern—shutting everything down for two weeks in July or August—is in great part a response to TSC, since summertime is when workers and their children can vacation together. YRS, by dispersing vacations around the year, should make it easier for industry to operate year round. Although few service industries and retail stores close down during the summer, their lot would also be easier if the entire work force was not trying to vacation during July and August. One might conclude that it is more rational and better for business to space vacations over the entire year.

There are surely exceptions to this rule. For instance, it is generally held that TSC developed so that farm children could work during the busy summer months. Therefore, YRS opponents argue, YRS may be unacceptable in rural areas. As is usual with YRS issues, this is only a supposition; we lack the facts needed to determine to what extent a YRS program might interfere with the operation of the family farm. Do farm children help out on the farm during the summer because they are available then or because that is when their help is most needed? Planting and harvesting time mostly occur during the TSC school year. The flexibility of YRS could be used to adapt school vacation to the requirements of farm life. Let rural communities determine what works best for them.

YRS will have other important effects on business. For example, in Miami, Florida, the tourist industry's peak demand for part-time help falls in the middle of the TSC school year. By making high school students available to work in tourist businesses from December to April, YRS benefits both industry and students who need to work. To take another example, the New England ski industry has also supported YRS, not only because it makes student employees more readily available, but also because YRS vacation schedules smooth out the peaks and valleys of the ski business. YRS reduces the jam of skiers on weekends and during Christmas week. The ski industry gets a more even demand placed on its facilities, and the customers get less crowded slopes, shorter lift lines, and lower mid-week prices.

A recent Gallup Poll on education[4] found that 80 percent of the public favored more emphasis on career preparation in high school. YRS can facilitate career education by making on-the-job experiences easier to schedule. An on-the-job experience in TSC disrupts either the educational process or the employer. The school must find a way to adapt classes to work hours. The employer must arrange for jobs that are less than eight hours a day and less than a full year long. A YRS program, in contrast, can assure that a job will be full-time for one vacation session. Thus an employer can create one full-time position through which three to five students will cycle during the year. A full-time position, since it can be made a more integral part of the firm, should provide a more meaningful job experience. Another advantage of a full-time on-the-job experience is that it more realistically exposes the student to the demands of the world of work than does a day that is half spent in school and half spent at work.

The discussion so far in this section illustrates an important point about YRS: school planners should not neglect the opportunity YRS brings of tailoring school vacations to their community's needs. However, YRS may have effects beyond the local business community. The household moving industry supports YRS because it would change the pattern of when families move. Currently, more than 60 percent of all household moves take place during the three-month summer vacation. YRS would more evenly spread moving throughout the year and would thus permit the moving industry to provide more stable employment for its workers and better service to its customers. As a result, the costs of moving would decline.

To be sure, YRS raises problems for the summer camp industry. It is not clear what will happen to the demand for summer camps when the three-month summer vacation is eliminated. Attendance may decline. On the other hand, YRS would present the opportunity for more efficient use of camp facilities by establishing year-round camps rather than just summer camps.

In many communities, a variety of agencies—such as the YMCA, church programs, and recreational facilities—operate special summer programs for vacationing school children. YRS can have major consequences for these programs. Although the summer demand for such services will be less, a year-round demand will be created. Many agencies might find it to their advantage to operate programs all year long, rather than to face a summer peak and then a complete loss of school-aged children for the remaining nine months of the year. For example, Boy Scout or Girl Scout camps could operate in the spring and fall as well as in the summer, serving more children with the same facilities.

In general, recreational facilities would benefit from YRS. If vacation periods were spread more evenly through the year, the peak demand on most recreational facilities would be reduced, and usage would be more stable, providing better income for the employees. The U.S. Forest Service carried out a study of future expected use of the recreational facilities of the National Parks and U.S. Forests. The study concluded that the only way the rising demand for leisure activities in the National Parks by the year 2000 could be met was for the entire country to convert to YRS so that vacations would be spread from April to October instead of being concentrated in June, July, and August.[5]

*YRS and Larger Social Problems*

The effects of YRS on the community are not restricted to meeting the needs of industry, making vacations more pleasant, or providing part-time jobs for students. YRS programs, with their multiple graduation times, have additional benefits for society. TSC, by dumping all its graduates onto the job market at one time, swells the number of unemployed. In most industries, new workers are needed throughout the year, not only in the last week of May. As a result, many recent high school graduates remain unemployed for long periods of time until industry can gradually absorb them. The full extent of this psychologically destructive and socially wasteful problem is hidden by the unemployment figures released by the Department of Labor, which are seasonally adjusted to smooth out unemployment peaks that are consistent from year to year. While the full costs of this system are not obvious, one can wonder about the relationship between the rise in crime during the summer and the number of unemployed high school graduates TSC dumps on the community every June.

Juvenile crime may be affected in other ways by YRS. There is some (sketchy) evidence to suggest that school vandalism declines over the summer months if school buildings are in use. Apparently a deserted building is a tempting target. Perhaps some juvenile crime is the result of the boredom and frustration that a long, hot summer vacation brings about; YRS will thus help reduce juvenile delinquency by shortening and redistributing vacation periods.

To take another tack, YRS can be used to facilitate school

desegregation. School buildings, after all, wear out and must be rehabilitated or replaced. The physical facilities in worst shape are usually ghetto schools, which, although initially well-constructed, are often 50 to 100 years old and in need of replacement. Rather than build a new ghetto school and then bus children in and out of that school to maintain racial balance, the school district could close the old school, change nearby schools to YRS, and redistribute the students from the closed school to the YRS schools. The savings involved would be particularly welcome, since communities must bear the cost of busing and of police protection for students.

Many communities must deal with the problem of providing an education to the children of migrant farmworkers. Always on the move, migrant children rarely complete a normal school year. The benefits that a well-planned YRS program can bring to migrant children can be best illustrated by an actual case. In this particular school district, migrant families move into the area in May, remain through the summer, and move out in late October. Before YRS, the migrant children were bused to schools all over the district and were placed in whatever class had room for them. When the regular school year ended in June, they had a brief vacation and then attended a six-week summer session at their neighborhood school. After another brief vacation, when regular school resumed in the fall, the migrant children were again bused all over the district but after a month or so moved on with their families.

This inadequate system is characteristic of migrant education. However, the school district changed to a 45-15 calendar. Now the migrant children attend their neighborhood school for the entire time they live in the district. They are placed in a group scheduled to start shortly after the families move into the district. After the end of the 45-day session, the migrant students are free to attend a special "inter-session" (vacation school) during the three weeks their regular school group has vacation. They then attend a second regular 45-day school session. In this way, the migrant children have a continuous, well-integrated educational experience that allows them to complete about 145 days of the state's required 175 days of attendance.

## Conclusions

This chapter has at least touched on many of the issues raised when a school district converts to YRS. Those considering the possibility of changing to YRS should consult the works included in the bibliography; they should also get in touch with the National Council on Year-Round Education. Another good source of information on the effects of YRS is the California Department of Education, which requires schools receiving state aid in changing to YRS to conduct evaluation studies during the first, third, and fifth years after the change.

# 5

## The Federal Government and YRS

In the United States the responsibility for education is given to the states by the Constitution. Nevertheless, the federal government has from time to time undertaken a variety of programs to encourage and support educational programs. The land grant colleges gave considerable impetus to the growth of postsecondary education. Veterans' education benefits, the Guaranteed Student Loan Program, Basic Educational Opportunity Grants, and the National Defense Education Act have directly involved the federal government in financing college education. The Title I program provides special additional educational experiences for disadvantaged students in elementary school, as do other programs aimed at migrant children, bilingual students, and the handicapped. Other federal programs have helped build buildings, develop libraries, and produce Sesame Street and the Electric Company. In short, although education may be the responsibility of the states, federal involvement in education has been extensive.

There seems to be sufficient precedent for Congress to play a role in either encouraging or discouraging the spread of YRS at some point if YRS becomes a national issue. While Congressional action may be a consequence if YRS becomes a political issue, there is another reason why Congress should pay some attention to the present YRS movement. As presently structured, the YRS movement is a local, grass-roots development. Individual, local schools are facing and making the choice between YRS and TSC on the basis of local concerns and issues. But, as was shown in Chapter 4's discussion of YRS and the community, a large-scale adoption of YRS would have ramifications throughout society. It does not seem wise for the federal government to sit idly by and let change of national scope be brought about as an accidental by-product of local decisions based on local concerns. Further, Congress may find that it is in the national interest to encourage local schools to change to YRS. Questions of the most efficient scheduling of employee vacation time, overcrowding of the national parks, and many others are issues of national concern that may be affected by YRS.

In addition to the variety of its programs directly or indirectly providing educational services, the federal government is the primary source of money for educational research. By and large, the issues addressed in educational research transcend the narrow concerns of a local school and often require resources beyond those available to the local school. Since the results of research benefit all schools and since the federal government can make resources available by collecting a small amount of tax from each school district's population, the federal government is in an ideal situation to be the nation's chief purveyor of educational research.

Schools considering YRS as well as those who have changed from TSC to YRS are greatly in need of research on YRS. Parents, teachers, and administrators have many questions: how much money will YRS save; will the children be psychologically damaged; will achievement test scores go down; will family and community life be disrupted? Many schools, through feasibility studies and evaluations, have attempted to provide answers to some of these questions. However, the limited resources available to local schools to conduct research have left most of the questions about YRS unanswered. Only the federal government has the resources to carry out the research needed to answer the many questions raised about YRS.

We have seen that YRS raises a multitude of questions that can, and should, be answered by research. We have seen that YRS is a major educational innovation that already affects many students and is under active consideration in many more schools. Indeed, when both the number of students and the sweeping, across-the-board changes (as in curriculum) associated with YRS are considered, it seems fair to say that YRS is one of the most important educational innovations in the United States today. We have seen that the federal government plays the major role in conducting educational research in the United States and that there is considerable need for research on YRS. With this background, the reader will be surprised to know that until 1975, the federal research offices had paid absolutely no attention to YRS. In 1975, the Office of the Assistant Secretary for Planning and Evaluation (ASPE), of the Department of Health, Education, and Welfare (DHEW) conducted two very small studies of the status of YRS and in 1976 began the largest study of a YRS program ever conducted. These efforts amount to about one one-thousandth of all the resources the federal government devotes to educational research. The National Institute of Education (NIE), the federal agency most responsible for research into educational innovations, contributed about 8 percent of the money for the ASPE study, or some .02 percent of NIE's annual budget. The public is not well served when the nation's chief education research agency ignores such an important educational innovation and the often-voiced need of the public for research answers on what YRS is all about.

**Awareness of YRS in Washington, D.C.**

The federal education establishment's apparent lack of concern and interest in one of the major educational developments of the day struck us as puzzling, so we made a brief effort to learn more about it. The federal education "establishment" is made up of three parts: (1) Congress, especially the committees that deal with education; (2) agencies in the executive branch that operate education programs and carry out educational research; and (3) Washington representatives of various educational organizations—the education lobby. To find out what the education establishment knew about YRS, in mid-1975 Abt Associates staff discussed YRS with a number of officials.

Of the federal officials contacted, although all were acquainted with the concept of year-round schools, none had more than a limited knowledge of specific YRS programs currently in operation nor a clear idea of the potential of YRS. Officials at the Office of Education and NIE were aware that YRS is frequently implemented as a solution to school district fiscal and overcrowding problems, but all were skeptical of its success in these areas. In the area of curricular innovation, they displayed ignorance of exactly what YRS can accomplish as they cited supposed drawbacks. Specifically, they believed that YRS automatically accelerates students through school and thereby creates a whole series of social problems—15- and 16-year-old high school graduates, strains on the job market, and implications for the retirement age.

When the disadvantaged child and YRS were discussed, these federal officials could see no greater role for the government and their particular educational agencies than to act as a national repository of research, evaluation, and documentation data in the area of YRS and the disadvantaged child. Not having considered the potential implications YRS has for the disadvantaged child and for the various federal compensatory education programs, they saw only a tangential relationship between YRS and the responsibilities of their offices.

The representative of the Council of Chief State Officers was only minimally acquainted with even the concept of YRS. However, he warned against the dangers of increased truancy and vandalism in YRS (district YRS data do not support this claim) and the demands YRS would make on day care and community recreation providers. He did touch on one important aspect of any educational innovation—good community relations.

At the National Association of Secondary School Principals (NASSP) the interviewee was generally unimpressed with the potentials of YRS. He maintained that YRS did not save money because capital costs are a small percentage of the total budget of a school, especially as a long-term expenditure (6-10 percent), and operational costs rise with YRS. He stated that "anybody who thinks that schools aren't used all year just doesn't know what they're talking about." He added that there is already tremendous wear-and-tear on facilities—there are many more people per square foot in elementary and secondary school buildings than in even the poorest college and in most office buildings. Finally, he could see no benefits to the disadvantaged child in YRS.

The person spoken to at the National Education Association (NEA) was probably the most informed about YRS since she had written an information packet on YRS for NEA a year ago. She believed that YRS had not proven itself to be a money-saver and that interest in YRS was waning. While she felt that YRS potentially held some benefits for teachers—extra pay and increased status as professionals with a longer teaching year—she was also concerned with the possible problems YRS would create for teachers. She cited a reduction in the number of teachers employed, time/pay abuses, contract/tenure changes, and dangers to long-term benefit accrual as among these possible problems.

These discussions suggested to us that, for the most part, policy makers in Washington are not well-informed about YRS. Their opinions on YRS, based on misinformation or lack of information, are generally unenthusiastic and frequently unfavorable. These federal officials and individuals in educational organizations seem not to be interested in YRS.

In sharp contrast, local and state educators display increasing interest in YRS. One individual active in YRS states that weekly he receives dozens of telephone and mail inquiries about his district's program. Interest has become so great that he has set aside an afternoon each week to take interested administrators, teachers, and parents on a prearranged tour of the program. A consultant to the California Department of Education who provides technical assistance to schools planning YRS programs said that interest is so high that he assists several new schools with their planning each month.

It seems that the federal education establishment is at least five to eight years behind the times in YRS. Why has the federal education establishment missed the emergence of YRS as one of the most sweeping and widespread developments in education in recent years? Probably the major factor contributing to the lack of federal interest in and knowledge of YRS is that YRS grew as a grass-roots response to local issues and was not directly related to what were considered national education issues in the decade from 1965-1975. There is a tendency for the federal education establishment to only pay attention to "national" issues. In general, this is a sensible way to proceed—the federal government should be concerned with national issues while grass-roots concerns should be left to local government. But this division of labor doesn't work when educational research is the issue. After all, the federal role in research is to provide resources for research on matters of concern at all levels. However, the pervasive focus on national issues among federal policy makers tends to influence the federal educational researchers.

Another source of the federal education establishment's overlooking YRS may be found in the nature of YRS's innovations. YRS is different from other innovative programs in that a majority of if not all the other educational innovations developed over the past two decades assume a 180-day school calendar followed by a summer vacation. A number, most notably Head Start, used the summer as the time in which to assist educationally deprived and economically poor children prepare for the traditional calendar. However, most federal programs such as Title I projects, Educational Vouchers, Performance Contracting, and Follow Through, were designed for use during the traditional school year.

The second major difference is in the source of funding. While there have been some federal monies invested in YRS, YRS has neither been generally funded nor supported in any major way by the federal government. Contrarily, most of the major educational innovations of the past few decades have been federally funded, supported, and initiated as well.

Another major difference between YRS and other innovations is in its buttressing philosophy, if not ideology. Specifically, most innovations were developed with a single goal in mind: to help the disadvantaged child. Although these programs may have had varying goals (cognitive, affective, or psycho-motor development, or combinations of these) they were child-centered innovations. The theory said that if additional educational assistance could be given at an earlier age, if parents had a choice, if teacher/child ratios increased, or if the most advanced technology could be applied, then the various goals would be reached. YRS, on the other hand, seemed to be based on a community need—saving taxpayers' dollars—and secondarily concerned about accelerating achievement or social growth. In recent times data have indicated that YRS may be an intervention strategy that does indeed have an educational impact. Instead of cost savings alone, more and more YRS adherents are turning to the potential and sometimes documented effect of their programs on students.

## YRS and Federal Research and Development

An Overview of how the federal government spends its policy research monies is relevant at this point. YRS's current status in the federal educational research and development (R&D) program can be appraised using the simple classification illustrated in Table 5-1. While there is some question about the number of students enrolled in YRS programs, even the restricted definition we have used allows us to estimate that the number is about one million. Hence, YRS projects, a large-scale phenomenon under the control of Local Education agencies (LEAs), fall in Cell III. A glance at the other cells will give perspective.

Table 5-1
Federal Research and Development Projects

| | Locus of Control | |
| Size of Program | Within LEA | Outside LEA |
| --- | --- | --- |
| Small | I | II |
| Large | III | IV |

Small projects controlled by LEAs (Cell I) are those funded by Title I and III of the ESEA. The LEA devises a small innovation and then receives some grant-in-aid money for it. However, systematic evaluations are usually performed by states (most of them are systematic monitoring efforts or part of large-scale evaluation studies under Title I and III). Though such programs are generally well-documented, the ad hoc evaluative designs often do not involve LEAs to any substantial extent. These evaluations are used by federal policy makers and legislators and only secondarily by LEAs.

Most university projects would be found in Cell II. They are devised by academic researchers for purposes of improving peda-gogical techniques or the state of the art in methodology. Adequate evaluation is usually performed, because of the university base; but once again, LEAs do not look to these programs for much help in trying to change their systems. Cell II projects also depend on outside funding—usually foundations and sometimes the federal government. The major difference between Cells I and II is that in Cell I the LEA usually controls or devises the innovation; this is not true of Cell II. However, they are similar in that assessments of each are performed, usually in a systematic manner, by someone not involved in the day-to-day operations. In short, Cells I and II usually are well-documented. There is empirical evidence that reflects what happened.

Cell IV programs share with those of Cells I and II the presence of an evaluation component. Typical programs would be Educational Vouchers, Performance Contracting, and Experimental Schools. They are large programs devised by other than LEAs and are systematically evaluated.

Within this classification scheme, Cell III is unique: evaluations and program research are usually done willy-nilly, at best. Thus, their importance is transmitted without the benefit of systematic and objective information. YRS is one of the best examples of programs in this category. YRS programs are large-scale and have been initiated and controlled by LEAs. As previously noted, their assessment is left to either an anecdotal process or to small studies of individual programs that are not comparable or not evaluated.

While the federal government has, as mentioned, displayed an interest in YRS, the major conclusion reached—as a result of exploring YRS and its relationship to other projects and programs in the federal R&D context—is that DHEW needs to expand its current role. A rational R&D policy would certainly not miss the opportunity to systematically examine a locally initiated innovation as widespread as YRS. Further, given ASPE's mandate to examine projects and programs concerned with the educationally and economically disadvantaged, a YRS research agenda becomes even more urgent. Finally, YRS should be tested and assessed with respect to its potential in solving a wide range of current social problems (i.e., desegregation and unemployment problems of youth).

In conclusion, then, there definitely is a role for the federal government in YRS research; the federal education research agencies have not been meeting their responsibilities in this area. It also seems that Congress should pay some attention to those aspects of YRS that raise national issues.

# 6

## Should Your Community Consider YRS?

To a large part of American adult society, our present educational system is a "mystery wrapped in an enigma," if not an active source of discomfort. Communities throughout the United States are erupting in heated political debates about busing and school closings, about what books should be read by their children and whether a new school bond issue ought to be passed. In some instances, these debates have even resulted in pitched battles involving angry parents, police, and students.

Whether the debate or the battle of the moment is over busing, segregation, neighborhood schools, or raising taxes, it is clear that the issues surrounding public education are increasingly controversial. Neighbor pitted against neighbor, school board member against school board member, and community against the federal government—especially the federal courts—these are a few of the contestants involved. In each of these instances it is clear that there is no single answer. Federal court decisions differ from one district to another. Some communities, who a year or two ago would have bragged about their neighborhood schools, have now voted to close one or two as an economy measure.

Given this political climate, where does YRS fit? How can it help? Should it be considered in Boston or Louisville? Does YRS have the potential for affecting neighborhood schools, school closings, and desegregation? We believe so. Not that YRS will solve all your community's educational ills. But reviewing the history of other communities as they considered, adopted, and reflected on YRS is instructive. Judging by their experiences, you may conclude that YRS in fact has great potential for helping to solve a particular educational problem.

As we said in the preface, we do not wish to be viewed as advocates for YRS. However, we do advocate that your school district or community study group examine YRS as a way to solve some of your more pressing educational problems. The process of assessing the desirability and feasibility of YRS can itself be enormously helpful.

For example, if Winchester, Massachusetts had adopted YRS, its Wyman School might still have had to close—tax and revenue problems might have persisted anyway. However, if the community had been investigating educational innovations and ways to save money—to get a bigger educational bang for their buck—they would at least have run across YRS as one systematic way of dealing with costs and savings. Further, they would have found examples of hundreds of communities that, when confronted with rising costs and scarce resources, had seriously considered YRS. Even those that vetoed YRS learned from its approach to the problem of costs. And in a larger sense, communities that grappled with the potential impacts of changing the school calendar—impacts on children, families, institutions, and the community itself—learned from this analysis of the school system.

As noted throughout, most of the conclusions one might reach about the impact of YRS on children and costs are tentative. However, there are strong indications, strong directions in the extant information. For instance: there are probably substantial savings involved when at least a YRS option is implemented in a school district; if a YRS option is offered in one of the schools of a district it will be an integrated school; and finally, children's summer vacation learning loss may be avoided. A definite need exists for more systematic research, but given the strong directions of our findings, YRS warrants serious consideration by any community facing the range of educational issues described above.

Should your child be in a year-round school? We don't know. We would need to know more about you and your child, about your community and your view of the future. We do know that YRS, as a grass-roots educational movement, has assisted millions of Americans struggling with the expensive and difficult task of teaching their children how to read and write.

# Appendix A
## Geographic Location of YRS Districts

The following maps represent the growth and location of year-round school programs across the country: Figure A-1: Year-Round School Programs, 1973; Figure A-2: Year-Round School Programs, 1975; and Figure A-3: Year-Round School Programs, by Model, 1975.

The data used in Figure A-1 were taken from *Year-Round Education in the United States*, Trenton, N.J.: New Jersey Department of Education, 1973. The data appearing in the remaining figures were collected from *Year-Round Education Activities in the United States*, Trenton, N.J.: New Jersey Department of Education, 1975, which covers the period from July 1, 1974 to February 1, 1975.

Because of our slightly restricted definition of a year-round school program, we omit a few programs listed in these sources (e.g., Fairview School District, Pa., an operational plan listed as "summer semester voluntary"; and Millcreek Township School District, Pa., in the preimplementation stages of "two terms plus summer").

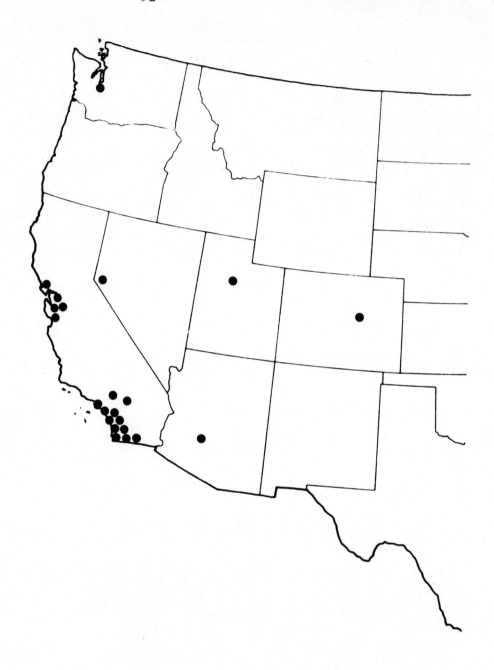

**Figure A-1.** Year-Round School Programs, 1973.

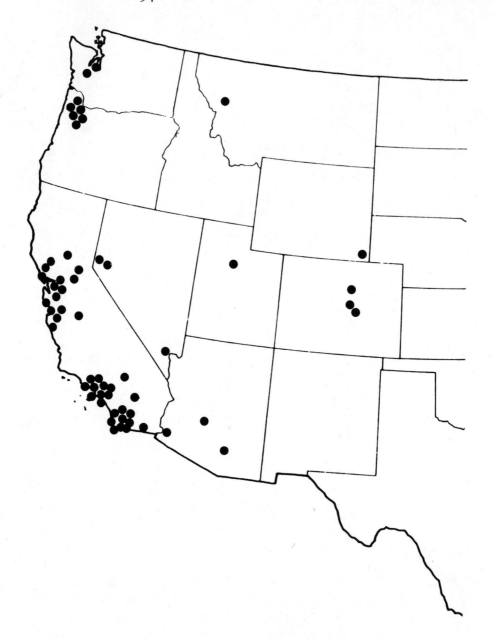

**Figure A-2.** Year-Round School Programs, 1975.

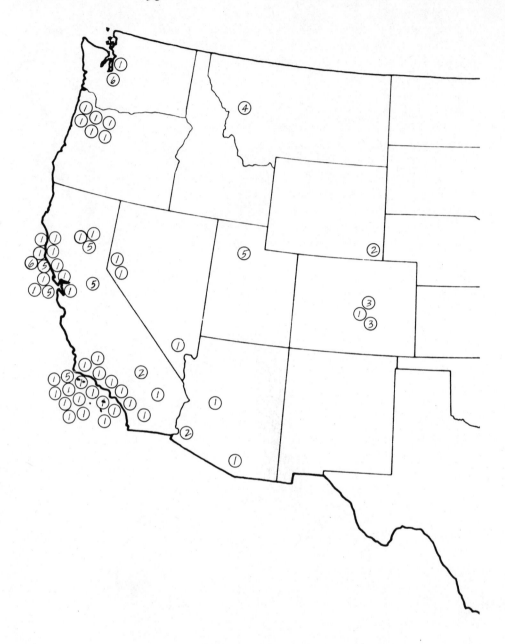

**Figure A-3.** Year-Round School Programs, by Model, 1975.

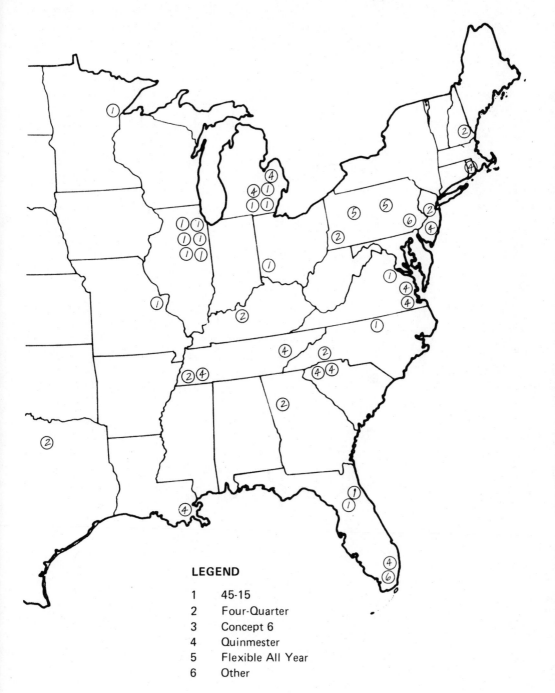

**LEGEND**

| 1 | 45-15 |
|---|---|
| 2 | Four-Quarter |
| 3 | Concept 6 |
| 4 | Quinmester |
| 5 | Flexible All Year |
| 6 | Other |

# Notes

# Notes

## Chapter 1
### Year-Round Schools from the 1800s to the Present

1. George Glinke. *The Year-Round Education Movement: Its Historical Implications on Today's Urbanized Culture*, Utica, Mich.: Utica Community Schools, 1970, p. 7.

2. Ibid., p. 8

3. Ibid., pp. 8-9

4. Ibid., pp. 11-12.

5. *Year-Round Schools: Models and Issues*, National Council on Year-Round Education, May 1975.

6. Glinke, op. cit., pp. 5 and 16.

7. Ibid., p. 25.

8. Ibid., p. 27.

9. Ibid., p. 26.

10. Ibid., p. 29.

11. *Encyclopedia of Education*, S.V. 4th ed. "YRS in Fairfield, Connecticut."

12. Glinke, op. cit., p. 42.

13. *Setting the Stage for Lengthened School Year Programs*, Albany, N.Y.: the University of the State of New York/The State Education Department, 1968, p. 10.

14. *Year-Round Education Activities in the United States*, Trenton: N.J.: New Jersey Department of Education, 1975.

## Chapter 2
### The Current State of Year-Round Schools

1. *Year-Round Education Activities in the United States*, Trenton, N.J.: New Jersey Department of Education, 1973-1975.

2. Quoted in California State Department of Education. *A Summary of Year-Round Education in California as of November, 1974*, Sacramento, Calif.: Office of Program Planning and Development, 1974, p. 9.

Chapter 3
The Recorded Impact of Year-Round Schools

1. Paul D. Rice, David J. Parks, and Donald E. Parks. *A Bibliography and Review of Selected Evaluation Reports and Studies on Year-Round Education*, National Council on Year-Round Education, May 1, 1975, p. 132.

2. Ibid., pp. 132-133.

3. *Francis Howell Year-Round School Opinionnaire Summary*, November 1974, pp. 1-2 (mimeo).

4. *Third Evaluation Report, Park Elementary School*, Hayward, Calif.: Hayward Unified School District, March 1974, Part II, p. 5a.

5. Dwain Thatcher and Roslyn Grady. *Second Operational Year Report of Concept 6 Year-Round School*, Colorado Springs, Colo.: Colorado Springs School District Eleven, July 1975, pp. 28-30.

6. Ned S. Hubbell and Associates. *Attitudes Toward Year-Round School in Loudoun County, Virginia*, Port Huron, Mich.: Ned S. Hubbell and Associates, April 1975, pp. 27-29.

7. *Excerpts from Evaluation Reports of the Prince William County Year Round School Program During the First Year of Operation*, Manassas, Virg.: Prince William County Schools (n.d.).

8. *An Assessment of Attitudes Toward the LaMesa-Spring Valley School District Year Round School*, LaMesa, Calif.: LaMesa-Spring Valley School District, 1972, pp. 6-7.

9. Division of Instruction. *Rationale—Status and Direction of the Quinmester Program*. Miami, Fla.: Dade County Public Schools, February 1972, p. 13.

10. Thatcher and Grady, op. cit., pp. 16-20.

11. L.R. Moortgat. *A Study of Achievement and Absenteeism in the 45-15 Year-Round School Plan and Traditional Calendar Plan in the Northville Public Schools*, Northville, Mich.: (n.d.), pp. 31-32.

12. Conversation with Dr. Arthur Welch, Director of Planning, Loudoun County Public Schools, Manassas, Virginia.

13. *Third Evaluation Report, Park Elementary School*, Hayward, Calif.: Hayward Unified School District, March 1974, Part III, pp. 1-14.

14. *Evaluation of the Year Round School*, Hesperia, Calif.: Hesperia School District, (n.d.).

15. *Year Round Schools: An Assessment of the Program's Initial Year in Four Chula Vista Elementary Schools*, Chula Vista, Calif.: Chula Vista School District, November 1, 1972.

16. Education Turnkey Systems, Inc. *45-15 and the Cost of Education*, Washington, D.C.: Education Turnkey Systems, Inc., (n.d.).

17. Ernest H. Mueller. *Energy Consumption Comparison*, Prince William Co., Virg.: Prince William County Public Schools, 1973.

18. *A Research Design for Year-Round Education*, Virginia Beach, Virg.: Virginia Beach Public Schools, April 1973.

## Chapter 4
## YRS Issues Refined

1. Since a how-to-do-it manual can be of great use in guiding the work of YRS planning groups, we recommend John McClain's *Year-Round Education: Economic, Educational and Sociological Factors*, Berkeley, Calif.: McCutchan, 1973, which clearly and succinctly enumerates the steps in conducting a YRS cost analysis.

2. T.C. Thomas and S.H. Pelavin. *Patterns in ESEA Title I Reading Achievement*, Menlo Park, Calif.: Stanford Research Institute, March 1976.

3. R.L. Hamson, "Year-Round School: Political Football or Taxpayer's Dream?" Paper presented at the Annual Meeting of the Operations Research Society of America, Western Section, 1976.

4. G. Gallup. "Eighth Annual Gallup Poll of the Public's Attitudes Toward the Public Schools," *Phi Delta Kappan*, vol. 58, no. 2, October 1976, pp. 187-201.

5. E.L. Shafer, G.H. Moeller, and R.E. Getty. *Future Leisure Environments*, Upper Darby, Penn.: Northeast Forest Experimental Station, 1974.

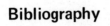

**Bibliography**

# Bibliography

## Evaluative and Feasibility Studies

*California*

Big Bear Lake, Bear Valley Unified School District, Ralph R. Bell, District Superintendent. *Implementation of Year-Round Education.* A simulation notebook presented at the 6th National Seminar on Year-Round Education. 1974.

Chula Vista City School District. *Year-Round Schools: An Assessment of the Program's Initial Year in Four Chula Vista Elementary Schools.* 1972.

Corona Norco Unified School District. "Evaluation of Corona Norco Unified School District Year Round Plan." 1973 (mimeo.).

Corona Norco Unified School District. Austin M. Mason, Assistant Superintendent. Form letter. Undated.

Corona Norco Unified School District. "Presenting the Extended Year Program." Undated.

Corona Norco Unified School District. *YRS and You.* Printed flier. Undated.

Elk Grove Unified School District. Nelson C. Price, Project Evaluator. *Secondary Program for Year-Round School, End of Project Report.* 1974.

Elk Grove Unified School District. *Secondary Program for Year-Round School Appendices, Project No. 1168.* 1974.

Hayward Unified School District, Robert H. Williams, Director of Elementary Education. "A Feasibility Study for a Four-Quarter Elementary School Year." Undated.

Hayward Unified School District. Raymond G. Arveson, Superintendent, *Third Evaluation Report, Park Elementary School.* March 1974.

Hesperia School District. *Evaluation of the Year-Round School.* Undated.

LaMesa-Spring Valley School District, Program Planning and Public Information. "Contract Information for Certified Personnel in Year-Round Schools." 1973.

LaMesa-Spring Valley School District. *An Assessment of Attitudes toward the LaMesa-Spring Valley School District Year Round School.* 1971-1972.

LaMesa-Spring Valley School District. "Cost Analysis: Year-Round School." 1972.

LaMesa-Spring Valley School District. *Evaluation Data: Year-Round School.* 1973.

LaMesa-Spring Valley School District. *Evaluation of Scholastic Achievement in the Year-Round School.* 1973.

LaMesa-Spring Valley School District. *Evaluation of Scholastic Achievement in the Year-Round School 1972-1973.* 1974.

LaMesa-Spring Valley School District. Howard B. Holt, "A Secondary School Staff Evaluates Its Year-Round Program." 1972 (mimeo.).

LaMesa-Spring Valley School District. *Second Annual Year-Round School Attitudinal Survey.* 1973.

LaMesa-Spring Valley School District. *A Visual Summary of LaMesa-Spring Valley School District's Year-Round School Attitudinal Survey.* 1972.

LaMesa-Spring Valley School District. "1974 Parent Opinion Survey Results." 1974.

Watsonville, Pajaro Valley Unified School District. "Continuous Learning Through Year-Round Schools." Undated.

Watsonville, Pajaro Valley Unified School District. *Year-Round School Evaluation, First Year Report.* 1974.

Watsonville, Pajaro Valley Unified School District. *Year-Round School Report: End of Third Year.* 1975.

Sacramento, State Department of Education, Office of Program Evaluation and Research and Office of Program Planning and Development. *Evaluation Instrument for School Districts Operating Year-Round Education Programs in California.* 1975 (mimeo.).

Sacramento, State Department of Education, David Sweet, Don Glines, and Bob Ehlers, principal writers. *A Summary of the Evaluations of the Year-Round School Districts in the State of California, June, 1971-June, 1974.* Undated (mimeo.).

Sacramento, State Department of Education, Office of Program Planning and Development. *A Summary of Year-Round Education in California as of November, 1974.* 1974 (mimeo.).

Sacramento, State Department of Education, Don Glines, YRE Consultant. *Year-Round Education Practices Survey Results.* 1975.

*Colorado*

Colorado Springs School District Eleven. Dwain Thatcher and Roslyn Grady. *Second Operational Year Report of Concept 6 Year-Round School.* July 1975.

Colorado Springs, El Paso County School District #11. *Year-Round School Concept 6.* Undated.

Jefferson County School District R-1. "Concept Six Background Information," *Jeffco Concept 6* (multibrochure information packet). Undated.

*Florida*

Fort Lauderdale, Broward County School Board, John E. Arena, Ellen Hannan, Edgar C. Perry, David Rubin. *The Learning Activity Package: What It Is and How to Use It.* Undated.

Miami, Dade County Public Schools, Division of Instruction. *Cost Analysis of the Quinmester Program.* 1972.

Miami, Dade County Public Schools, Division of Instruction. *The Quinmester Plan in Dade County Schools: A Progress Report.* 1973.

Miami, Dade County Public Schools, Division of Instruction. *Rationale—Status and Direction of the Quinmester Program.* 1972.

Miami, Dade County Public Schools, Division of Instruction. *Status Activities—Direction of the Quinmester Program.* 1972.

Miami, Dade County Public Schools, Division of Instruction. *Status and Projections—Quinmester Program.* 1974 (mimeo.).

*Georgia*

Atlanta Public Schools. Jarvis Barnes, Assistant Superintendent, Division of Research and Evaluation. *Evaluation of Fourth Quarter: Research and Development Report.* Volume VIII, No. 3, December 1974.

Atlanta Public Schools. E. Curtis Hensen, Administrative Director of Research and Federal Projects. *The Four-Quarter Program in Secondary Schools.* 1974.

Atlanta Public Schools. E. Curtis Hensen. "Work Experience and Year-Round Education." Undated.


*Illinois*

Naperville Community School District #203. *A Feasibility Study on the Year-Round School, 1972-73.* Undated.
Romeoville, Valley View School District #365. James R. Gove, Superintendent. *Feasibility Study of the 45-15 Plan for Year-Round Operation of a Public High School Served by an Elementary District Already on the 45-15 Plan, Final Report.* Submitted to USDHEW/OE. 1972.
Romeoville, Valley View School District #365. *Information Fact Book.* Undated.
Romeoville, Valley View School District #365. A. Vito Martinez, Division of Educational Services. "A School Board President's Thoughts on the Valley View 45-15 Continuous School Year Plan." Undated.


*Michigan*

Northville Public Schools. L.R. Moortgat. *A Study of Achievement and Absenteeism in the 45-15 Year-Round School Plan and Traditional Calendar Plan.* Undated.
Northville Public Schools. Raymond E. Spear. "Year-Round School on the Move—From Challenge to Implementation." 1975 (mimeo.).
Northville Public Schools. David Ogg, Frederick R. Ignatovich. *Validation Report, Parts I, II, III.* 1975.
Northville Public Schools. *Year-Round School: Is It Acceptable?* Undated.
Northville Public Schools. *Year-Round School: Is It Feasible?* 1970.
Northville Public Schools. "45-15 ESY." 1973.
Utica Community School District. Phillip Runkel, Superintendent. *The Four-Quarter Staggered School Year: A Feasibility Study to Extend the School Year—A Research Study.* Utica, Mich.: Utica Community Schools, July 1970. (Includes Glinke, George, "The Year-Round Education Movement: Its Historical Implications on Today's Urbanized Culture.")

Utica Community School District. Don Bemis, Superintendent of Schools. *The Optional Five-Term Year-Round Educational Plan: A Step Toward Implementing Plans for Extending the Regular School Year—Phase II, The Communications Phase.* 1971.


## Minnesota

Mora, Independent School District #332. Russell Mills, Lawrence Nelson, James Revier, Jeff Saari. *Assessment of the Feasibility of Continuous Secondary School Year Independent School District #332.* 1974.


## Missouri

St. Charles County, Francis Howell School District. *Francis Howell Year-Round School Opinionnaire Summary.* 1974.
St. Charles County, Francis Howell School District. "Francis Howell Year-Round School Questionnaire Summary." 1972.
St. Charles County, Francis Howell School District. Alan M. O'Dell, Elementary Education, compiler. *Francis Howell Year-Round School Plan.* 1972.
St. Charles County, Francis Howell School District. Alan M. O'Dell, compiler. *A General Report on the Francis Howell Year-Round School Plan.* 1972.


## New Hampshire

Hudson School District, Alvirne High School. *Course of Studies, 1973-74, 1974-75.* Undated.
Hudson School District, Alvirne High School. *Results of the Alvirne High School/University of Idaho Secondary Student Professional Staff and Lay Citizen Attitude Questionnaire.* 1974.
Hudson School District, Alvirne High School. *The Steckevicz-Alvirne Quarter Plan as Designed by Chester J. Steckevicz.* Undated.


## New Mexico

Roswell Independent School District. *Annual Report of Title III ESEA Extended School Year Study.* 1973.

Roswell Independent School District. *Year-Round School Study and Curriculum.* Undated.


*New York*

Albany, University of the State of New York and the State Education Department, George I. Thomas, Coordinator. *Setting the Stage for Lengthened School Year Programs.* 1968.


*Oregon*

Molalla Consolidated Grade School District #35. Joe Morton. "Molalla Keeps Schools Open All Year Long." *Salem, Oregon Statesman.* April 21, 1971.
Molalla Consolidated Grade School District #35. Web Ruble. "Year-Round School Plan Called Success by Molalla." *Portland Oregon Oregonian.* January 31, 1972.


*Pennsylvania*

Fallsington, Pennsbury School District. *Feasibility Study: Cooperative Planning for a Flexible School Year.* 1974.


*Virginia*

Leesburg, Loudoun County Public Schools. Ned S. Hubbell and Associates. *Attitudes Toward Year-Round School in Loudoun County, Virginia.* 1975.
Leesburg, Loudoun County Public Schools, Planning Department. *45-15 Program Status Report.* 1974.
Prince William County Public Schools. *An Educational Choice.* 1974.
Prince William County Public Schools. Education Turnkey Systems, Inc. (Washington, D.C.). *45-15 and the Cost of Education, Summary.* Undated.
Prince William County Public Schools. Ned S. Hubbell and Associates. *Attitudes Toward Year-Round School.* September 1972.

Prince William County Public Schools. Ernest H. Mueller. *Energy Consumption Comparison.* 1973.

Prince William County Public Schools. *Excerpts from Evaluation Reports of the Prince William County Year Round School Program During the First Year of Operation.* Undated.

Prince William County Public Schools. University of Virginia Bureau of Education Research. *Final Project Report on YRS Achievement of Prince William County Schools.* October 1972.

Virginia Beach School District. *The Effect of the 45-15 Pilot Project on Community Services in Virginia Beach, Virginia.* July 1974.

Virginia Beach School District. *The Planning and Preparation Phase of the Virginia Beach Pilot Program of Year-Round Education.* April 1973.

Virginia Beach School District. "A Public Information Approach." April 1973.

Virginia Beach School District. *A Research Design for Year-Round Education.* April 1973.


## Speeches, Seminars, and Monographs

Arkansas, Fayetteville School District, Arkansas School Study Council. *Mount Sequoyah National Seminar on Year-Round Education.* 1969.

Colson, John G. "Effects of Year-Round Schools on Teacher and Administrator Attitude and Performance." Paper presented to First Annual Mid-South Educational Research Association Convention: 1972.

_____. "Staff Attitudes and Performance in Year-Round Schools." Paper presented to First Annual Mid-South Educational Research Association Convention, New Orleans: 1972.

Figg, Jerry W. *A Community Survey.* A simulation notebook presented at the Sixth National Seminar on Year-Round Education, Chicago: April 30-May 3, 1974.

Hanson, R.L. "Year-Round School: Political Football or Taxpayer's Dream?" Paper presented at the Annual Meeting of the Operations Research Society of America, Western Section: 1976.

Heller, Melvin P. *The Extended School Year: Evaluation and Pitfalls.* A simulation notebook presented at Sixth National Seminar on Year-Round Education: April 30-May 3, 1974.

Jensen, George. "The Calendar—Underdeveloped Educational Resource." Speech presented to Third Annual National Seminar on Year-Round Education, Cocoa Beach, Fla.: 1971.

_____. "Effects of Year-Round Education on Business, Industry and the Professions." Paper presented to First Annual Mid-South Educational Research Association Convention: 1972.

Knight, Louise. "Year-Round Education." 1974 (mimeo.).

McLain, John. "Major Thrusts for Year-Round Education." Paper presented at Second National Seminar on Year-Round Education, Clarion, Penn.: April 1970.

_____. "Life Style, Living Patterns and the Year-Round School." Paper presented at the Fourth National Seminar on Year-Round Education, San Diego: 1972.

_____. *The Operation of the Flexible All-Year School Plan.* A simulation notebook presented at the Sixth National Seminar on Year-Round Education: April 30-May 3, 1974.

Mueler, Ernest H. *Feasibility Study—Fiscal Baseline.* A simulation notebook presented at the Sixth National Convention for Year-Round Education, Chicago: April 30-May 3, 1974.

National Council of Year-Round Education. *2nd National Seminar on Year-Round Education.* Harrisburg, Penn.: April 5-7, 1970.

_____. *3rd National Seminar on Year-Round Education.* Cocoa Beach, Fla.: March 24-26, 1971.

_____. *4th National Seminar on Year-Round Education.* San Diego, Calif.: February 23-25, 1972.

_____. *5th National Seminar on Year-Round Education.* Virginia Beach, Virg.: May 8-11, 1973.

_____. *6th National Seminar on Year-Round Education.* Chicago: April 30-May 3, 1974.

_____. *Year-Round Schools: Models and Issues.* (Prepared under DHEW Contract #SA-4997-75 to NCYRE, by Rice, Paul D.; Olsen, J.I.; Parks, David; and Parks, Donald.) Washington, D.C.: ASPE/DHEW, May 1975.

Olsen, Johannes, and Rice, Paul. *Do We . . . Or Don't We . . . Have to Change the Instructional Program for Year-Round Operation.* A simulation notebook presented at 6th National Seminar on Year-Round Education, Chicago: April 30-May 3, 1974.

Parks, David J. and Parks, Donald E. "Interest Groups and Year-Round Schools in California, 1973-74." 1975 (mimeo.).

_____ and Leffel, Linda. "Needed Research in Year-Round Education." Paper presented at 1973 Annual Meeting of the American Educational Research Association: 1973.

Root, Barbara. *Staff Inservice.* A simulation notebook presented at 6th National Seminar on Year-Round Education, Chicago: April 30-May 3, 1974.

Rubenstein, Martin. *The Development-Status of the Dade County Quinmester Program.* A simulation notebook presented at the 6th National Seminar on Year-Round Education, Chicago: April 30-May 4, 1974.

Vanderzanden, Gail Y. *Dissemination of Information about Year-Round School Operation.* A simulation notebook presented at 6th National Seminar on Year-Round Education, Chicago: April 30-May 3, 1974.

Whiteley, Alfred C. *Student Scheduling in a Year-Round Middle School.* A simulation notebook presented at 6th National Seminar on Year-Round Education, Chicago: April 30-May 3, 1974.

Worner, Wayne M. *Feasibility Study—Educational Baseline.* A simulation notebook presented at the 6th National Convention for Year-Round Education, Chicago: April 30-May 3, 1974.

## Pamphlets, Books, Handbooks, and Articles

American Camping Association. "How to Think about the Extended School Year." Martinsville, Ind.: 1971.

Bernstein, Irene N., and Freeman, Howard E. *Academic and Entrepreneurial Research.* New York: Russell Sage Foundation, 1975.

Brieder, Calvin. "Year-Round Schools Raise Some Big Questions." *Nation's Schools,* 90, October 1972: 18.

California, Sacramento, State Department of Education, Office of Program Planning and Development. *Year-Round Education Handbook,* 1975.

California, San Diego, Superintendent of Schools. *Year-Round Education and the High School,* 1973.

Howe, Paul H. "Year-Round School Makes Good Business Sense Says This Boardman-Businessman." *American School Board Journal,* 160, February 1973: 46-48.

Jensen, George. "Let's Update Our School Calendar." Pamphlet printed as public service by Twin City Federal Savings and Loan, Minneapolis. Undated.

_____. "Why Not Kill the Root of the Summer Overload?" Pamphlet reprinted from *Mayflower Warehouseman*. Undated.

McLain, John. *Year-Round Education: Economic, Educational and Sociological Factors*. Berkeley, Calif.: McCutchan, 1973.

National Education Association. "Year-Round Schools and the Teacher." *Briefing Memo*, 5, Washington, D.C., 1974.

New Jersey, Trenton, State Department of Education, Office of Program Development, Henry J. Pruitt, Extended School Year Programs. *Legislative Activities Affecting Year-Round Education in the United States*. 1974.

Pascoe, David D. "Do We Really Want a Solution to Our Housing Problems?" *AESA Journal*. Los Angeles, vol. XIII, no. 1, February 1972.

Punke, Harold H. "Accountability and the Quarter System." *Bulletin of the National Association of Secondary School Principals*, January 1973: 57-63.

Rifkin, N.S. "A Round-Up on Year-Round Schools." *Today's Education*, 63, November 12, 1973: 58-64.

_____. "How to Make the Switch to Year-Round Education Schools." *American School Board Journal*, 160, February 1973: 40-46.

United States. 92nd Congress. House. Commission on Education and Labor. General Subcommittee on Education. *Year-Round Schools*. Washington, D.C.: April 24, 1972.

Varner, Sherrell E. *The Rescheduled School Year*. National Education Association, Washington, D.C.: 1968.

Williams, Roy E. "All Year School Part II, The Secondary School Picture." *AESA Journal*, Los Angeles, vol. XIII, no. 2, April 1972.

## Bibliographies and Directories

California, Sacramento, State Department of Education, Curriculum Services Unit. *California State Directory of Year-Round Education*. 1975 (mimeo.).

_____. *National Reference Director of Year-Round Education*. 1975 (mimeo.).

California, Sacramento, State Department of Education, Office of Program Planning and Development. *California State Directory of Year-Round Education*. 1973.

_____. Robert E. Ehlers, consultant. *Directory of Year-Round Schools.* 1974.

National Council on Year-Round Education. *Individual Membership List.* Clarion, Penn.: 1975 (mimeo.).

_____. *A Bibliography and Review of Selected Evaluation Reports and Studies on Year-Round Education.* May 1, 1975. HEW/OS/ASPE/EP Contract #SA-2997-75 to NCYRE by Rice, Paul; Parks, David; and Parks, Donald.

_____. *Annotated Bibliography on Year-Round Schools.* IPD Doc. 74-3. Washington, D.C.: 1974.

New Jersey, Trenton, State Department of Education, Division of Research, Planning and Evaluation, Bruce Campbell, compiler. *Year-Round Education Activities in the United States: First Annual Survey of State Education Agencies Concerning Activities, Including Legislation, in Year-Round Activities in the United States.* 1973.

_____. *Year-Round Education Activities in the United States: Second Annual Survey of State Education Agencies Concerning Activities in Year-Round Education in the United States.* 1974.

_____. *Year-Round Education Activities in the United States: Third Annual Survey of State Education Agencies Concerning Activities in Year-Round Education in the United States.* 1975.

# Index

# Index

# About the Authors

**Morris A. Shepard** is a free-lance policy research consultant and writer. During the past decade, he has taught at the Pennsylvania State University, been a senior evaluation analyst for the Office of Economic Opportunity, and most recently an area manager at Abt Associates in Cambridge, Massachusetts. He is the author and coauthor of numerous technical reports funded by all levels of government. He received the B.A. from Kent State University in Ohio and the M.A. and Ph.D. in Political Science from the University of Connecticut.

**Keith Baker** is a social science analyst in the Office of the Assistant Secretary for Planning and Evaluation, Department of Health, Education, and Welfare. He has also worked on the evaluation staff at the Office of Economic Opportunity and taught at the Pennsylvania State University. In addition to publishing articles in several journals, Dr. Baker is co-author of *Prison Education* and *Comprehensive Services to Rural Poor Families.* He received the B.A. from Miami University and the M.A. and Ph.D. in Sociology from the University of Wisconsin.